CLIMB
AGAINST
THE ODDS

+CLIMB+
AGAINST THE ODDS
Celebrating Survival on the Mountain

By THE BREAST CANCER FUND with MARY PAPENFUSS

CHRONICLE BOOKS
SAN FRANCISCO

The Breast Cancer Fund
2107 O'Farrell Street
San Francisco, California 94115
www.breastcancerfund.org

Page 160 constitutes a continuation of the copyright page.

Library of Congress Cataloging-in-Publication Data available.

ISBN 0-8118-3481-6

Manufactured in China.
Designed by Susan Park
Edited by Jessica Hurley

Distributed in Canada by Raincoast Books
9050 Shaughnessy Street
Vancouver, British Columbia V6P 6E5

10 9 8 7 6 5 4 3 2 1

Chronicle Books LLC
85 Second Street
San Francisco, California 94105

www.chroniclebooks.com

This book is dedicated to the women who reached beyond themselves mentally, emotionally, and physically and climbed against the odds. They climbed to rejoice in their courage—the courage they found when breast cancer made them face their own mortality. They climbed to demonstrate their commitment to a world in which cancer is a thing of the past. They climbed to raise awareness and funding for programs of education, support, and advocacy. Ultimately, they climbed, and will continue to climb, to give voice and presence to the eternal flame of hope in the human spirit. This book was written to honor the women who inspired the journey and whose precious lives were lost along the way:

EXPEDITION INSPIRATION
+ Laura Evans 1949–2000

MT. MCKINLEY
+ Marcy Ely-Wilson 1948–1999
+ Michele Potkin 1958–2000

MT. FUJI
+ Betty Burch-Riley 1940–2002
+ Deborah Ann Cohen 1961–2001
+ Rosa Meneses 1952–2000
+ Cheryl Ryan 1961–2002

CONTENTS

ACKNOWLEDGMENTS

A foggy pilgrimage along Fuji for
the Applied Materials team

Over one hundred women and men climbed against the odds to change the way we think and act about breast cancer. We at The Breast Cancer Fund, on behalf of all who have faced breast cancer, extend our deepest appreciation to these climbers and to all those whose contributions brought this book to fruition.

We thank the climbers for sharing their stories that continue to inspire the work at The Breast Cancer Fund, and especially thank the many women who shared their personal writing and offered us a more intimate glimpse into the experience of the climb. The incredible courage, strength, and perseverance of each climber moves every reader to reach for greater heights within one's self.

Thanks also go to James Kay, Lex Fletcher, Luis Garcia, Naomi Darling, Katie Gamble, and Alan Kearney for creating the photographs that made this book come to life, and for capturing the moments on the mountains with such beautiful and distinct skills.

We are grateful to the team of writers and editors who spent many long hours on this project. To Mary Papenfuss, we offer our appreciation for her bold steps in writing the stories. Catherine Flaxman's vision and support were vital to turning a great idea into the book we have before us today. And the final product could not have been delivered without the hard work and patience of Sarah Malarkey, Anne Bunn, and Jodi Davis of Chronicle Books, or Jessica Hurley's diligent editing.

A special thanks goes to Farmers Insurance Group for their generosity, and to the ongoing support of Clif Bar Inc., Amgen, Inc., Isis, and Avalon. With the generous support of these sponsors, the publication of *Climb Against the Odds* is made possible. We also thank all our outdoor sponsors for sustaining our remarkable climb expeditions.

Two members of The Breast Cancer Fund's staff deserve special recognition for their tireless coordination of the book, Esperanza Torres and Anna Hauptmann. Many staff and volunteers labored to ensure that these stories are shared with the public and kept alive for generations, most notably Nancy Evans, Merijane Block, Joan Reinhardt Reiss, Janet Nudelman, Megan Fowler, Jim Carroll, Iris Lancaster, H. L. Ittner, Diane Grunes, and Roberta Fama.

Finally, and most deservedly, we will always be grateful to Andrea Ravinett Martin, founder and executive director from 1992–2001, for her vision and determination to shout from the mountaintops that we can end the breast cancer epidemic by taking one step at a time.

JEANNE RIZZO,
Executive Director
The Breast Cancer Fund

INTRODUCTION

"To those who have struggled with them, the mountains reveal beauties they will not disclose to those who make

Climb Against the Odds: Celebrating Survival on the Mountain is about ordinary people facing extraordinary challenges. It celebrates women of grace and power who have faced an internal mountain—breast cancer—and have gone on to scale formidable peaks. Their stories reveal the link between the challenge of facing one's mortality and the challenge of aspiring to the summit of a mountain. The heroes of The Breast Cancer Fund's expeditions share their inspiring acts of daring, dedication, and determination as they encounter the physical, emotional, and spiritual experiences of the healing journey.

Climb Against the Odds is a photographic exploration of three majestic peaks and the climbers who scale them. The section on Mount Aconcagua (22,800 feet) in the Argentine Andes, the highest mountain on earth outside of the Himalayas, chronicles the two-week expedition of seventeen breast cancer survivors. In the second ascent, climbers scaled Mount McKinley (20,300 feet) in Alaska, referred to as "The High One" by Native Americans; and in the third, they climbed Japan's mysterious Mount Fuji (12,400 feet), home to spiritual pilgrims for centuries. The photographs on these pages are a tribute to survival, mountaineering, and the power of teamwork.

The idea to climb Mount Aconcagua with women who had experienced breast cancer came from Laura Evans, who, when diagnosed with advanced breast cancer, was on the path to becoming an accomplished mountain climber. The bone marrow transplant Evans received as primary therapy in 1989 interrupted her plans for a first climb of Mount Kilimanjaro, led by Peter Whittaker, her mentor and son of the first American to summit Mount Everest, Lou Whittaker.

Introduced to me by a mutual friend shortly after I founded The Breast Cancer Fund, Evans asked The Fund to serve as the nonprofit arm of the expedition—to help organize, promote, and fund-raise for the climb. She presented her idea with commitments from Whittaker, to provide professional guidance on the mountain, and Paul Delorey, president of JanSport, to donate the costs of the climb, tents, and backpacks.

Despite the fact that none of us had ever climbed a mountain, the Board of Directors of The Breast Cancer Fund was immediately receptive to the proposal. It had great potential to accomplish a lot of good by providing a unique way for women to turn their courage earned from fighting breast cancer to a challenge of their own choosing, to

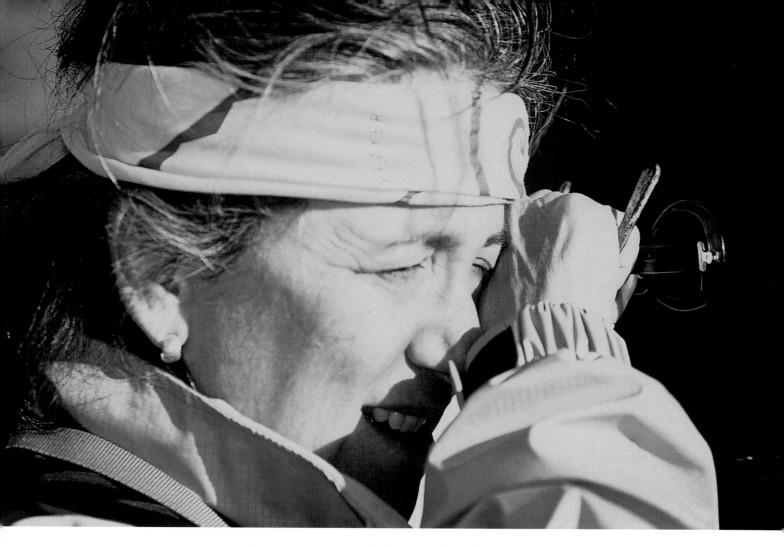

increase awareness and education about the disease within a strong message of hope, and to raise funds needed for research, education, advocacy, and patient-support projects.

Working with Evans and Whittaker and generously assisted by JanSport, The Breast Cancer Fund spent the next year and a half selecting, training, and outfitting a seventeen-member team, who together with the guides, several physicians, and a film crew formed the core of a forty-two-person expedition. The logistics of moving that many people from the United States to South America, up one of the world's tallest mountains, and safely back home were impressive, as was the variety and amount of mountaineering equipment donated to the effort by dozens of outdoor sports companies.

In addition to being one of the best-dressed and most well-equipped expeditions to ever climb a mountain, we were among the best trained. The team ranged in age from twenty-two to sixty-two. The only six with previous altitude experience were designated to attempt the summit, with the remainder of us playing the role of support. There were many practice climbs, including one on Mount Rainier, and hours spent in the gym and hiking local hills. In February 1995, all of us reached higher than we'd ever been before. For me, an exerciser but not an outdoorswoman, I exceeded my expectations in one of the most empowering experiences of my life.

Andrea Ravinett Martin sheds tears of joy after finishing her Fuji summit

Because of its many breakthroughs in raising hope, awareness, and funding for the fight against breast cancer around America and abroad, and because women shouting from a mountaintop are heard, climbing expeditions became a hallmark of The Breast Cancer Fund. A second expedition to the treacherous and windswept slopes of Mount McKinley was undertaken three years later. This time the climbers consisted of five who had faced breast cancer and seven young women who were determined to eliminate the disease from their futures.

In August 2000, The Breast Cancer Fund took a team of seventy-eight Americans who were joined by four hundred Japanese women, men, and children—all cancer survivors, their families, and their physicians—to climb the awakening volcano Mount Fuji, and left a legacy of hope and strength, energizing the newly emerging patient–advocacy movement in Japan. On each expedition, climbers carried prayer flags to the summit in tribute to all who have endured breast cancer. The flags, and the climbers who carried them, affirm the pledge to eradicate breast cancer so that mothers, daughters, sisters, and those to come may be free of cancer.

Through teamwork these women found the strength to overcome the challenges they faced from the treatments they had to endure as cancer patients and the harsh realities of reaching for a summit. Just as the climber leaves the security of base camp to undertake her quest for the peak, the cancer patient leaves behind the person she was and the life she knew prior to her diagnosis. By going high on the mountain, the climber reaches out for the same strength that the cancer patient calls upon to get through diagnosis, treatment, and recovery, moment by moment, step by step, breath by breath. In facing the unknown, each of these heroic women wrestled with demons of weakness, doubt, and fear that threatened her progress. Wind, ice, snow, heat, and altitude were indifferent to their desires. But whether the summit was attained or denied, the mountain taught that success lies in the journey, not just on the summit.

The women returned, forever changed, sustained by the depth of their experience and the passion of their teammates and supporters. Empowered and emboldened, they are prepared to move mountains in the quest to end the epidemic of breast cancer.

I am forever indebted to each and every climber who helped realize our dreams of shouting from the mountaintops to change how we think and act about breast cancer. From my early conversations with Laura Evans, to my first step on Mount Aconcagua, to carrying my own prayer flag up to the summit of Mount Fuji, this has been an incredible journey.

The wind carries our prayers of love, healing, and remembrance.
May we all be well.

ANDREA RAVINETT MARTIN,
Founder, former Executive Director,
and member of Board of Directors,
The Breast Cancer Fund

PART **1**

ACONCAGUA

+

EXPEDITION INSPIRATION

CHAPTER 1

THE FIRST STEP

LAURA EVANS

Laura Evans, a freelance fashion designer from Sun Valley, Idaho, spent years biking, hiking, and running half marathons. It was friend and legendary mountain guide Lou Whittaker who first convinced her to test her physical prowess on the high rocks. The initial trek up Mount Rainier in 1983 was a transforming experience for Evans, even though it ended abruptly when the new climber snapped her ankle while leaping across a mountain chasm. Though it would be another year before she would finally get to experience a summit's quiet communion, Evans was hooked on the sport upon her first ascent. She discovered that lessons don't only come with summits. "In the mountains, I had learned about priorities and interdependence," Evans wrote. "I had learned about the body and mind's ability to push beyond. I had learned that the bond of friendship forged in a life-threatening situation is stronger than any other."

By 1989, Evans would define herself as a mountaineer. "Everyone should be passionate about something," she wrote in her autobiography, *The Climb of My Life*. "Each one of us should discover and pursue that one, driving, I-cannot-live-without-it desire. For me, it is climbing mountains, both literally and figuratively."

Soon, Evans would need all her determination to meet a different type of challenge head-on. At age forty, she had just returned from a 250-mile hike through Nepal and was preparing for a climb up Mount Kilimanjaro in Africa when she discovered a marble-sized lump in her right breast while showering. Her physician assured her it was nothing to worry about. "I heard what I wanted to hear," Evans would later tell friends. However, within months she discovered a second lump in her right armpit. This time, she had a biopsy of the mass in her breast. As she awoke from anesthesia, Evans wrote, "I looked at Dr. Jensen, the one who had sent me home three months earlier. He had been so confident then. He would not look at me now."

Laura Evans had a deadly, fast-growing cancer that had infiltrated eleven of her lymph nodes, a strong indication that it was already spreading elsewhere. She was given a 15 percent chance of surviving the next three to five years. The climber had a mastectomy, intensive chemotherapy, and a bone marrow transplant, which was highly experimental at the time. For two months she lived isolated in a sterile hospital room while all the bone marrow in her body was systematically destroyed, then replaced. She was bald,

Opposite: The essential Laura Evans smiling at the prospect of reaching the 22,000 foot summit of Aconcagua

nauseous, weak, racked by pain, and vulnerable to debilitating infection. "On bad days I stared forlornly at the calendar on the wall, at all the empty days and meaningless Xs, afraid I would never leave that room, womb, tomb," Evans wrote. Often in her mind were the mountains. "Would I ever scale them again?" she wondered.

Eleven months after her treatment, Evans was determined to climb. This is not the plan that occurs to most breast cancer survivors, but Evans believed it was a way to vanquish the enemy within. She would prove her body was still strong, still hers to command, and that it could surmount anything nature could throw in her path. She summitted Mount Rainier the summer of 1992, followed by Kilimanjaro just four months later in October. Instead of hiking the last two hundred feet to the top of Uhuru Peak, she sprinted.

At some point, as she stood atop the highest point on the African continent, Evans had an idea. She told guide Peter Whittaker, Lou's son, that she would climb again, this time for breast cancer with other survivors. Whittaker dubbed the scheme "Expedition Inspiration" ("EI" for short), and he suggested Argentina's Mount Aconcagua—at 22,800 feet, the highest mountain in the world outside of the Himalayas. But they knew they couldn't meet this challenge alone. Evans reached out to another cancer survivor, and together they launched a movement that marked a sea of change in battling disease.

ANDREA RAVINETT MARTIN

Andrea Ravinett Martin enjoyed doing what people said couldn't be done. As a law student, she insisted on playing flag football on the Hastings Law School team. Martin played against men twice her size, until her head thumped so many times on the hard ground during one particularly brutal game that a concussion put her on the sidelines.

Years later Martin was told there was something else she couldn't do, at least not for much longer—live. She had been diagnosed with advanced stage-three breast cancer. "One doctor told me to go home and put my affairs in order," she recalled. "That's just what I needed to hear to decide to survive."

Martin discovered her breast cancer in 1989, when she was forty-two years old. Her daughter, Mather, was just six years old. Martin had married her second husband, Richard, the love of her life, only six months earlier. Two weeks before her diagnosis she had attended the funeral of her husband's forty-nine-year-old sister, who died of breast cancer. Martin's cancer was found in a biopsy of a lump in her right breast. Doctors had been watching the lump closely for three years; it had passed a mammogram screening just five months earlier.

Martin and her husband carefully researched treatment options and chose what, at that time, was known as a European method of chemotherapy, which entailed undergoing intensive chemotherapy before surgery. In this way, doctors could observe a

Andrea finds basecamp amidst
the stark landscape of Aconcagua

particular drug's effect on the tumor, and chemotherapy might immediately begin attacking cancer that may have already spread throughout the patient's body. This treatment regimen has since become far more common in the United States.

Martin endured grueling months of toxic drugs, the side effects of which were slightly tempered by visualization, acupuncture, herbs, and homeopathic medicines. The chemotherapy threw her into premature menopause, which eliminated the possibility of a biological child with her new husband and a sibling for Mather. The chemo regimen was followed by removal of Martin's breast and lymph nodes, more drugs, radiation, and finally another eight rounds of chemotherapy. "I went for second, third, and fourth opinions, hoping someone would tell me I didn't have to do that," she recalls.

Soon after healing from her year of treatment, Martin joined Dianne Feinstein's 1990 gubernatorial campaign and succeeded in raising millions of dollars, only to watch Feinstein lose the election by three percentage points. In 1991, just as Feinstein was beginning her bid for the U.S. Senate, Martin found a lump in her remaining breast. She was brushing her teeth with her right hand while using her left to engage in a popular pastime of breast cancer survivors—probing for new lumps. When her fingers found what she knew must be cancer, she was surprised at her reaction: "There was a layer of strength I hadn't had with the first diagnosis." Fortunately, it was a new primary cancer rather than

a far more serious metastasis, with none of the aggressive characteristics of the first cancer. Martin opted to have her left breast removed and began taking tamoxifen, an anti-estrogen drug that, in some women, prevents recurrence.

"Cancer profoundly changed me forever," Martin says. Her experience with cancer gave this survivor the resolve to follow a new path that led toward her career as founder and Executive Director of The Breast Cancer Fund in San Francisco, California.

THE FIRST MEETING

Two impressions struck Andrea Ravinett Martin during her first meeting with Laura Evans about Expedition Inspiration. The first was that Evans's plan was preposterous; the second was that she was hooked immediately. The bait was a tantalizing vision dangled by the driven athlete sitting across from Martin at the Airport Hilton in San Francisco. As light filtered through the bright fog beyond the hotel room window, Martin did little at first but listen as Evans talked sixty miles an hour, chugging Perrier and gesticulating with her hands while she outlined an idea that had grown into an obsession. It was the first time the two inspired women had met face to face.

As Martin watched Evans, she realized that people would call her scheme crazy. That's exactly what intrigued her. Martin wasn't a mountain woman. Though she stayed in reasonably good shape, she was not a fitness buff and had little experience sleeping in a tent. Nevertheless, she was drawn to Evans's vision. It was exciting and unique. It would be the first time in history that people with breast cancer would face such incredible physical challenges to raise awareness and funds for their cause. It would be a campaign that resounded with a public increasingly enthralled by the outdoors, physical challenge, and heroism. For the climbers themselves, the expeditions were to be a resurrection and a revelation, a way to meet what they were made of. These were intended to be comeback climbs, where women with breast cancer could shout victory from the world's highest peaks. But the climbs would bear startling similarities to the battle against breast cancer itself. They would be grueling ordeals overcome with support. They would be inspiring as well as terrifying, both hopeful and devastating—uphill battles in every way.

While Evans was the climber and the athlete of the new duo, Martin was the marketer. Though trained as an attorney rather than in marketing, she possessed a quick, innate sense of what would click with the public. Now she was ready to test her abilities to fight breast cancer with the organization she had only recently created. Evans's project was a bigger endeavor than she had anticipated undertaking, but Martin was prepared to give it a try. "I knew this climb would be the first time for anything like this. The entrepreneurial side of me wanted The Breast Cancer Fund to be the organization to do it," she says.

FROM PERSONAL TO POLITICAL: RAISING FUNDS AND AWARENESS

At the time when Evans and Martin started to organize the Aconcagua climb, "selling" a disease to raise public compassion and funds by capitalizing on the vigor and determination of people with the illness was a completely new phenomenon. Focusing public attention on any illness and keeping it there is a tough job, and it's even tougher for breast cancer. The healthy don't like to be reminded of disease and mutilation, particularly when it comes to something as crucial to the public libido as breasts. Americans like to see their breasts in cleavage, in commercials, TV series, magazines, and films—not in a jar in a pathologist's lab.

Public queasiness about breast cancer was dramatically demonstrated in the controversy that erupted following a graphic ad campaign launched by The Breast Cancer Fund. In January 2000, the "Obsessed with Breasts" ads, targeted for San Francisco and select Bay Area bus shelters, featured sultry, topless models with cascading curls and come-hither looks. The models had it all . . . except breasts. Scars across their chests (actually Andrea Ravinett Martin's mastectomy scars superimposed on the photographs) were apparently too much to bear in a city considered tolerant of nudity in performance art, sex clubs, and parades. Outdoor Systems, the company that manages bus-shelter ads in San Francisco, refused to run them. *San Francisco Chronicle* columnist Ken Garcia scoffed that trying to protect the city from a shocking sight on the street was like trying to protect the folks in Los Angeles from smog. A *Chronicle* cartoon showed a businessman thinking, "Shocking!" as he frowns at one of the ads, while behind him, giant advertisements hawk sex shows. The "Obsessed with Breasts" ads were quickly pulled in some cities.

Martin admits the ads, directed at our culture's most profound symbol of sexuality and nurturing, were shocking. But, she adds, "there's little advantage of perpetuating softened images of the breast cancer epidemic or its consequences. The more we shrink from the truth about breast cancer, the more women will suffer in silence and shame and the less we will be able to protect the next generation from its ravages."

Despite the obstacles, The Breast Cancer Fund had to win the hearts and minds of the public if any headway were to be made in the war against the disease. Each year hundreds of diseases vie for a limited pool of research funds; some manage to muster far more resources than their death toll would appear to merit. That has not been the case with breast cancer. Its toll in the United States is astounding:

+ A woman dies of breast cancer in this country every thirteen minutes.

+ Breast cancer is the leading cause of death for women between the ages of thirty-four and fifty-four.

+ Breast cancer accounts for one of every five cancer diagnoses.

+ The incidence of breast cancer has more than doubled among women in this country since the 1940s.

+ One of every eight American women will develop breast cancer at some time in her life.

+ More American women have died of breast cancer in the last twenty years than the number of Americans killed in World Wars I and II and the Korean and Vietnam Wars combined.

And yet, until recently, funds to fight breast cancer remained minuscule, particularly in relation to its toll. In 1990, only ninety million dollars was spent on breast cancer research. While the disease was responsible for 17 percent of cancer deaths that year, only 6 percent of available funds were spent on breast cancer research. Both Martin and Evans found the situation infuriating. Both women opted to make that which was personal, political—to make their battle with cancer a global war. "We were determined to call attention to a disease that had reached epidemic proportions and that was virtually being ignored," wrote Evans. Said Martin: "With my first diagnosis of breast cancer came fear. With my second, anger."

At the time the two women met, the breast cancer movement was in its infancy. Only a handful of other organizations had been launched, among them Massachusetts Breast Cancer Coalition in Boston, Susan G. Komen Foundation in Dallas, and Breast Cancer Action in San Francisco. The movement was built in part on tactics pioneered by AIDS activists, who were driven in desperation to agitate for funds and laws to battle the disease ravaging the gay community.

Like breast cancer, AIDS was a disease the public didn't care to be bothered with. In a call to action that resounded with the breast cancer community, playwright Larry Kramer wrote of AIDS in *The New York Native* in 1983: "This is our disease and we must take care of each other and ourselves." Gay activists provided a model for everyone with the disease by refusing to go quietly into that good night. They were in your face with angry street protests, drag sit-ins, and a controversial demonstration in St. Patrick's Cathedral that grabbed national attention. Like the Obsessed with Breasts ad campaign, the point was not to make the public comfortable. AIDS activists insisted on changing the label for people suffering from the disease. They were no longer AIDS victims. They were soon PWAs—People with AIDS—emphasizing that they were people just like everyone else, regardless of their sexual preference.

The cancer movement took that concept one step farther, referring to those with the disease as cancer survivors, and making them sound like what they are—heroes who have come through an ordeal, like concentration camp or earthquake survivors. The AIDS movement also introduced physical exercise in the form of a marathon walk to raise consciousness and a record amount of cash for the disease. The AIDS Walk, started in 1985, is a way to bypass government allocations and corporate foundations and go directly to people on the street for much-needed cash. Those concerned about AIDS can either walk to raise money or pay others to do the walking for them. It was a new twist on what at the time was one of the most famous fund-raising events, Jerry Lewis's telethon, which raised money for muscular dystrophy. Instead of Jerry and his celebrity pals pulling an entertainment marathon, AIDS walkers were hiking twenty miles. The event, held annually in cities across the country, repeatedly broke fund-raising records.

> "The mountain before me is one I did not choose to climb."

LAURA EVANS 1949–2000

Laura smiles all
22,800 feet of the way

After the Aconcagua project was launched, AIDS organizations established Climb for The Cure, mountaineering expeditions to raise funds for AIDS, as well as breast cancer. The Komen Foundation sponsors Race for The Cure, and in 1998, Avon began a three-day walk for breast cancer. The difference with Expedition Inspiration was that survivors themselves would do the work. They would make the struggle with life-threatening disease the kind of drama the public could admire and respond to. At the same time they could reap benefits of the climbs: develop a mental toughness to continue on after their illness, work to make their bodies stronger, and build a community of support for themselves and others with the disease.

Ultimately, the value of the climb was that it would successfully sell a concern about breast cancer to the public. These weren't women wasting away in hospital beds. These were warrior survivors climbing mountains.

PAUL DELOREY

Before Andrea Ravinett Martin would agree to work with Laura Evans on the climb, she had two conditions: first, Evans would have to delay the start of the climb for one year to give The Fund organizing time, and, second, the women would travel to the Outdoor Retailer Association trade show held in Reno that year to test the waters for sponsorship.

Evans picked Paul Delorey, whom she had known from her work as a fashion designer, as her first contact that day on the trade show floor. He was to be the first key

test in The Breast Cancer Fund's Aconcagua Expedition. Evans would always think of Delorey as Santa Claus, slimmed down and with a trimmer and bristly white-gray beard, an ever-ready smile, and a booming laugh. He would also be the bearer of a great gift for the project.

When Evans and Delorey had their first heart-to-heart about the Aconcagua climb, Delorey was managing JanSport, one of the biggest outdoor-equipment corporations in the nation. Company sales of backpacks and mountaineering equipment had doubled in five years, a testament to America's growing obsession with exercise, the outdoors, and increasingly demanding physical challenges. As Delorey checked the finishing touches on the JanSport exhibit, a massive display of colorful backpacks and clothing, Evans quickly outlined the plan for the Aconcagua climb. She asked if JanSport would be interested in helping bankroll the project. Delorey surprised her with one quick word: "Yes."

Evans knew, as anyone in the breast cancer movement quickly discovers, how pervasive the disease is, but she would continually be surprised at how wide a path of destruction the cancer burns and how personal the toll. There on the floor of the trade show, in the midst of commotion and a blur of color, Delorey discussed his own wrenching experience with breast cancer. Three cousins came to live with the Delorey family when he was just ten. He learned years later that their mother, his aunt, had died of breast cancer at the age of thirty-five. Few understood better than he did how one woman's death could have so many painful consequences.

CHAPTER ²
MEET THE TEAMS

+ TREK TEAM
SURVIVORS:

+ SUMMIT TEAM
SURVIVORS:
Claudia Berryman-Shafer
Vicki Boriak
Laura Evans
Nancy Knoble
Annette Porter
Mary Yeo

+ GUIDES:
Catie Casson
John Hanron
Heather MacDonald
Jeff Martin
Kurt Wedburg
Peter Whittaker

+ SUPPORT:
Dr. Bud Alpert
Paul Delorey
Andrea Gabbard
James Kay
Steve Marts
Jeannie Morris

+ TREK TEAM
SURVIVORS:
Claudia Crosetti
Eleanor L. Davis
Patty Duke
Roberta Fama
Sue Anne Foster
Sara Hildebrand
Nancy Hudson
Nancy Johnson
Kim O'Meara
Andrea Ravinett Martin
Ashley Sumner-Cox

+ GUIDES:
Larry Luther
Sue Luther
Mike "Ole" Olson
Ned Randolf
Mark "Tuck" Tucker
Jennifer Wedburg
Erika Whittaker

+ SUPPORT:
Bill Arnold
Dr. Ron Dorn
Roger Evans
Dr. Kathleen Grant
Byron Smith
Saskia Thiadens

THE SHAKEDOWN

With money pledges finally in hand, it was up to Evans to assemble her team. Hundreds of climbers and breast cancer survivors who had little mountain climbing experience contacted her after hearing of the unusual expedition through the cancer pipeline, including oncologists, therapists, friends, and members of support groups. Many others applied through ads in *Shape* magazine and other publications. It was up to Evans to whittle over two hundred applicants down to seventeen climbers. The women were selected on the basis of their experience with breast cancer, their physical ability to trek or climb, and their willingness to share feelings and insights with other team members and with the world in general through the media. The team members ranged in age from twenty-two to sixty-two, and included single and married women with and without children, some of them grandmothers.

In July 1994, the initial members of Expedition Inspiration gathered for the first time as a team on 14,411-foot Mount Rainier for a "shakedown climb." This climb would test the survivors' athletic aptitude and help determine who would be chosen to go all the way to the top of Aconcagua in January 1995. Eleven survivors, including Andrea Ravinett Martin, would made up the "Trek Team," which would provide support for the other survivors tapped to make the summit bid with Laura Evans.

THE TREK TEAM

CLAUDIA CROSETTI AND NANCY JOHNSON

Claudia Crosetti and Nancy Johnson of Ukiah, California, were the first team members to be selected by Evans. Crosetti had been diagnosed at age thirty-eight while working as an administrative assistant at the local junior college. During her recuperation she sought a support group, but, as she explains, "There weren't many breast cancer patients, just cancer patients in general. I think I would have benefited more if we'd had the commonality of body image and treatment issues."

In 1990, Nancy Johnson had recently moved into a new house in Ukiah with her partner of four years, Janet. An energy consultant, Johnson, who had grown up on a farm in the Midwest, led an active, healthy lifestyle. "In Illinois, when I was twelve, I worked

Opposite: The Aconcagua team

in the cornfields with other kids my age," she recalls. "We were sprayed with pesticides over a period of three summers. I often wonder how many of the other girls on my detasseling crew ended up with some kind of cancer. There is a high incidence of cancer in my hometown. Much of it has been traced to pesticide exposure."

Eventually Crosetti and Johnson met. "We both were into physical activity, such as playing tennis, running, race walking, swimming," Johnson says. "So we thought, why don't we do that together? We can talk about our cancer experience while we're doing physical things. We became our own support group, and later started a breast cancer support group in Ukiah."

Laura chose the duo for the team both for their shared passion for fund-raising and for their openness about discussing their breast cancer.

+ Eleanor Davis relaxes during a break from training

ELEANOR L. DAVIS

Eleanor Davis of Berwyn, Pennsylvania, was forty in 1979 when she discovered a lump in her breast. At that time, breast cancer was still very much "in the closet"; no one talked about it and mammograms were not routinely prescribed, nor widely available. After a mastectomy and a year of chemotherapy, doctors recommended a prophylactic mastectomy of Davis's remaining breast. "I decided to go ahead and do it," she says. "I really believe that's why I'm alive today—because I don't have any breast tissue left." After her surgeries and treatment, Davis finished the nursing degree that she had begun before her diagnosis. She immersed herself in raising her children, in her nursing career, and in working as a volunteer for the American Cancer Society to help other women.

At fifty-five, Davis was physically fit and had a lively sense of humor. She enjoyed golfing, skiing, and hiking, and had also climbed Mount Kilimanjaro in 1992 with her family. When she first heard about Expedition Inspiration she was hesitant to dredge up the past. "I sent for the application anyway, and after reading it, I realized that there would be a commonality, that we would speak of our experiences with no explaining needed," Davis says. "I knew I could speak about what chemo felt like, about the feelings of worry and fear of death, and the vulnerability that all of us experience. I knew there would be trust." She adds, "I hope that my length of survivorship gives others confidence about the future."

ACONCAGUA

Breathtaking Mount Aconcagua at 12,800 feet

"I choose to wear my scars."

NANCY JOHNSON

PATTY DUKE

Patty Duke was diagnosed with breast cancer in October 1992, when she was forty-three years old. A former model turned clothing designer for her company Smartwool, she was headquartered in Steamboat Springs, Colorado. Before the diagnosis Duke had led a very active life with her husband, Peter, and their two sons. "My encounter with breast cancer was what it took for me to slow down and take stock," she says. "The things I learned from the journey were valuable and enriching."

As a result of her cancer treatments Duke became afflicted with rheumatoid arthritis, and she often has to climb downstairs backward in the mornings because her ankles get so stiff. When she heard about Expedition Inspiration she applied, but because of her physical limitations she didn't expect to be chosen. When Evans told her that she had made the team, she says, "Peter and the boys had to peel me off the ceiling!" When asked why she wanted to take on this challenge, Duke says, "I climbed to reclaim my body after being bombarded with chemicals and radiation, to experience the wonderful women of Expedition Inspiration."

ROBERTA FAMA

At age twenty-six, Roberta Fama, a sales associate with Merrill Lynch in San Mateo, California, had been told for a year that she was "too young" to have breast cancer. Despite her strong suspicions, three mammograms, and a needle biopsy, doctors found nothing. Shortly after Fama's marriage to her longtime sweetheart, a second biopsy finally turned up cancer. "We wanted a big family and had already picked out their names," she says. "Everything was planned, except for the cancer. Upon my return from my honeymoon, I celebrated my twenty-seventh birthday and immediately had a modified radical mastectomy followed by six months of chemotherapy. Two and a half years later when I was trying to start a family, my back began to bother me. The cancer had metastasized in my back. It had eaten away three-quarters of my vertebrae and part of my rib was removed." A few years later doctors discovered a large cyst on one of Fama's ovaries and recommended a hysterectomy. Her plans to give birth were over, and she and her husband separated shortly after the surgery.

Fama had never been much of an athlete, but she wanted to do her part to fight breast cancer and hoped to join the climbing team because she wanted women to know that "even if cancer comes back, it doesn't have to be the beginning of the end."

At age thirty-four, Fama was one of the youngest team members. She trained for the climb with twenty pounds of kitty litter in her backpack. Jogging, walking on the treadmill, and hiking up hills, the litter was always rattling behind her like a rain stick, reminding Fama of the work she still needed to do to get in shape. She was petrified she wouldn't make the grade. Evans had everyone a little bit scared; she was nearly as hard on the climbers she had handpicked for Aconcagua as she was on herself.

When Fama found out hikers would be carrying forty pounds on the shakedown climb up Mount Rainier, she panicked. She called Evans and explained that her back was still sore from the surgery she had undergone for cancer in her spine. Naturally, Evans was frustrated that she hadn't been told of this condition earlier. Fama explained that her back wasn't bad, but that she was worried because her muscles had atrophied since the operation. Because of this, she came very close to backing out.

After her first hour up Mount Rainier, Fama was convinced that "no way" would she survive the hike. Yards from the summit, this survivor thought, "I'm going to die on this bloody mountain." Minutes later, perched at the top, Fama burst into tears.

SUE ANNE FOSTER

Sue Anne Foster, an art therapist, had been diagnosed with breast cancer in 1992, when she was forty-seven. "After a mastectomy, eight months of chemo, six weeks of radiation, and much inactivity, the climb was the first exciting and positive thing I had encountered related to cancer," she says. "I imagined how perfect this would be to help me focus on getting back into shape and reclaiming my body. Who would have thought that having breast cancer would be an asset on a résumé?"

Foster sent pictures of herself superimposed onto the team's promotional poster and also offered to be the team masseuse. "I think that cinched it," she says with typical dry humor. With her passionate dedication to natural health, vegetarianism, and social causes, Foster was affectionately dubbed the team's "hippie."

+ "Team masseuse," Sue Anne Foster, taking good care of her team

SARA HILDEBRAND

Sara Hildebrand had been jolted by her diagnosis of breast cancer in 1993, at age sixty. "Fritz [Hildebrand's husband] is a marathoner, so we eat a very healthy diet," she explains. "Exercise is part of our lifestyle. I had no cancer in my family, I was in perfectly good health." Hildebrand had trekked in Nepal in 1992 and climbed 19,300-foot Mount Kilimanjaro in 1990.

In 1994, five months after her mastectomy, Hildebrand applied to be part of the team. "There are some things in life you know you shouldn't do or you're not sure

Laura Evans and Ashley Sumner-Cox
give each other a congratulatory hug
at the end of the climb

you even want to do," she says. "With this, I really didn't hesitate. I was delighted to be able to put my energy into something positive."

NANCY HUDSON

In 1989, at the age of thirty-eight, Nancy Hudson was diagnosed with breast cancer. She had recently separated from her husband and worked as an art consultant, raised funds for local charities, and was busy raising her two sons. Hudson was diagnosed right after helping a close friend through her ordeal with breast cancer. "I had a modified radical mastectomy of my left breast," she reports. "The procedure left me devastated, distraught, and hollow."

When Hudson was forty-two, she joined Expedition Inspiration. She says, "It gave me the opportunity to turn a horrifying experience into one of the most positive, valuable, and life-altering events of my lifetime. I climbed to send a message to all women and men that there is life after breast cancer, and for all the women and men that have lost their loved ones to breast cancer."

KIM O'MEARA

Kim O'Meara, an athletic vegetarian with short-cropped brown hair, was known for her friendly, easygoing manner. She was fit and loved the outdoors, and even chose to trek with her husband, Art, in Alaska for their honeymoon.

O'Meara was probably the survivor most torn about her decision to join Expedition Inspiration. This was because the thirty-nine-year-old artist and teacher from Cedar Rapids, Iowa, would have to leave her four-year-old son, Evan, home while she challenged the mountain. It was thanks to him that O'Meara found her cancer as early as she did. Evan was just three months old when he began refusing to nurse from her left breast. Having found a mass in the breast, doctors attributed it to common changes due to lactation. However, O'Meara insisted on a biopsy and discovered she had a stage-two breast cancer tumor. She had a lumpectomy, six months of chemotherapy, and seven months of radiation. She nursed her new son for the last time right before undergoing surgery.

After she discovered her cancer, O'Meara says, "My goal was to see Evan turn one. Now every birthday I celebrate with him is a blessed, wonderful celebration." When asked why she joined the expedition, she says, "I climbed to be involved with an important, history-making, inspirational project that had the potential to achieve change."

ASHLEY SUMNER-COX

Ashley Sumner-Cox was only eighteen when she was diagnosed with breast cancer in 1991, and twenty-one when she joined the team. During her senior year in high school in Charlottesville, Virginia, she had a breast reduction. "I was a very active kid and I was tired of my breasts getting in the way all the time," she says.

A routine examination of the removed breast tissue revealed cancer. The doctor was astounded that he had found cancer in an eighteen-year-old, and sent tissue samples to six other doctors for confirmation. The unanimous recommendation was a mastectomy.

When joining the team, Sumner-Cox was afraid that "I was going to feel alienated because I was the youngest and not going to be able to interact very well with the team. I was afraid that the trek was going to be too hard and I wasn't going to be able to keep up. I had a whole lot of self-doubt. I talked about it to Laura and she reassured me. She also told me not to get any older." Evans understood the promotional value of having such a young breast cancer survivor on the team. Sumner-Cox joined the Trek Team in September 1994 and missed the Mount Rainier shakedown climb. She finally met the team in October, during another training session in Sun Valley, Idaho. Her self-deprecating humor and little-girl demeanor endeared her to the other team members, and she became the baby sister of the team.

TREK TEAM GUIDES AND SUPPORT

Accompanying the Trek Team would be guides Larry Luther, Sue Luther, Mike "Ole" Olson, Ned Randolf, Mark "Tuck" Tucker, Jennifer Wedburg, and Erika Whittaker. Dr. Ron Dorn; oncologist Kathleen Grant, M.D.; and nurse Saskia Thiadens (founder of the National Lymphedema Network) would climb to contribute medical support. Roger Evans would also join the crew to encourage the vision of his wife, Laura. Additionally, Bill Arnold and Byron Smith would be on hand to document the momentous journey on film.

THE SUMMIT TEAM

CLAUDIA BERRYMAN-SHAFER

Claudia Berryman-Shafer was a teacher living in Fernley, Nevada, with her husband, Jim, when she was diagnosed with breast cancer. If anyone could be called an Iron Woman on the expedition it was Berryman-Shafer, or "Claudia no B.S.," as she was called by her teammates. She had already summitted Alaska's Mount McKinley in the 1980s—twice. Four days after a mastectomy of her right breast in 1993 for a stage-two cancer at age forty-four, she ran a ten-mile race, taping the drains left from surgery to her chest. A big concern for Berryman-Shafer was how she would run the races she had planned before chemotherapy started. She ran them, finishing them only a bit "farther back in the pack than I used to."

Berryman-Shafer tackled the mountain the way she had tackled her cancer, aggressively and with high hopes. After all, she had a good role model. Her mother had

A pleased Claudia Berryman-Shafer at the shakedown climb on Mount Rainier

beaten breast cancer with a mastectomy thirty years before her daughter's diagnosis. "From the beginning, I had decided that cancer wasn't going to stop me," Berryman-Shafer says.

VICKI BORIAK

Vicki Boriak, thirty-nine, was a single mom with two teenagers. At the time of her diagnosis, she was an active outdoorswoman who worked for a sports company in Santa Cruz, California. She loved hiking, river rafting, and backpacking and thought she was the last person who would ever get breast cancer. But one night in August 1993, her boyfriend guided her hand to the spot: a pea-sized lump. Boriak immediately had a mammogram, but the mass didn't show up. "I told one radiologist that I could feel the lump and told him to feel it. He refused. He told me 'you are too young and fit to worry about it.'" She insisted on a biopsy, and her fears were confirmed. She had a mastectomy, and surgeons found two lumps in her breast.

"Many of us walk around under false pretenses that we're safe because we are healthy," Boriak says. "I used to look in the mirror and say to myself, 'You don't look like you have cancer,' as if cancer has a look. Cancer made me aware of my own mortality. All of us are going to die and none of us knows the circumstances of that death. The time to do what's important to you is now."

Boriak had finished chemotherapy just six weeks before the shakedown climb. "I had to make that climb, but I had a tough time convincing Laura," she says. "She didn't think I could do it so soon after treatment." Boriak wanted to climb to get her body back in shape and to intensify the experience of being in the moment. "There is no place I'm more in the moment than on a mountain. You dump all the mental chatter," she says. "There is nothing behind and nothing forward. You focus on one step, one breath. The clarity you achieve from an experience like that is astounding."

NANCY KNOBLE

A tall athlete with white-blonde hair from Tiburon, California, Knoble discovered her cancer in 1993. She had taken some time off from her job as vice president of human resources for Pacific Telesis to tend her ailing father. "One day I'm fine," she recalls. "I'm lying in bed, waking up. My father is alive. I'm back east in my parents' home. He is dying of cancer. I rub my hand across my chest and feel something. I knew that it shouldn't be there. It felt a lot like the prior benign breast tumor I'd had. It was kind of hard. It was kind of pea-shaped. It wasn't real big. I thought, 'You know, this is not the time to deal with this.' So I didn't do anything about it until after my father's death."

Shortly after her father died, Knoble and her husband were on a bike trip in Oregon when she told him she had found a lump. She remembers, "And he said, 'You did

Vicki Boriak makes a strenuous
crossing of the river during her ascent

what? You mean you didn't call the doctor the minute you found out?'" When her doctor told her it was nothing to worry about, Knoble insisted on a biopsy. She was diagnosed with stage-one breast cancer on her father's birthday, ten days after his death. She had a small tumor with no lymph node involvement. Knoble had the lump removed, followed by radiation therapy. In 1997, the cancer struck again and she had a bilateral mastectomy.

Nancy Knoble was an obvious choice for the summit team. She had climbed Mount Rainier in 1992 and summitted 18,500-foot Mount Elbrus in Russia a year after her breast cancer diagnosis. "I love the challenge. Climbing centers my thoughts and feelings, and helps me in everything else I do," she says. Knoble wasn't chosen for the team until well after the shakedown climb, but she says, "I knew I would be part of the expedition in one way or another. I knew I was meant to be part of it."

ANNETTE PORTER

Annette Porter of Surrey, United Kingdom, was thirty-two when she discovered a lump in her right breast that turned out to be invasive, ductal carcinoma that had spread to her lymph nodes. She had a lumpectomy and a year of chemotherapy and radiation—as she puts it, "matching aggression with aggression." One of the most emotional times during her treatment was her interaction with a key person in her life, her goddaughter Annie. Porter, who is single with no children of her own, was worried about how the little girl would react to her bald head and increasing pallor as she endured chemotherapy.

Typically, Annie would visit daily, and the two would cuddle and talk. After she lost her hair, Porter carefully covered her head with a scarf so she wouldn't frighten Annie. When the little girl asked to see Porter without the scarf, she removed it, but Annie was terrified and asked her godmother to put it back on. "Even though we talked about my baldness and her upcoming visit, there was nothing that could have prepared her for seeing her 'Netty' without hair. And there was nothing that could have prepared me for the pain I experienced when I saw that she, for the first time, was unsure of me. Gone was the naturalness of our relationship. Annie's instincts for self-protection led her to maintain a distance." Porter walked the docks near her house and cried, realizing, "This was going to be harder than I had ever imagined it would be." But little by little the two friends found their way back to one another. Porter had stopped sleeping in a scarf even though Annie was coming in to wake her up. "One morning, we had our usual round of stories, games, and goofy jokes," she recalls.

+ A sweet ending: Nancy Knoble and Vicki Boriak hold hands at the end of the trail

"Then she gave me her gift. She put her hands on my cheeks and looked into my eyes. Her mouth slowly turned up into a smile as she said to me, 'You know, Netty, you're the same old Netty, no matter what.'"

Porter had never set foot on a mountain, though she was an avid biker and skater. Yet as soon as she heard about Expedition Inspiration, she had to go. How tough could it be, she thought, when she had just beaten breast cancer? "Turns out, the thing I knew less about than breast cancer when I was first diagnosed, was mountain climbing," she says. She endured a grueling training year that included a shakedown climb up Washington's Mount Rainier. Despite the aching muscles, blistered feet, and painfully cold hands, she says, "I've learned that you're not given a challenge in life without the wherewithal to get through it. It's just that sometimes you have to look really deep to find it." She adds, "Climbing and fighting cancer are a lot alike. Something about working so hard to survive reminds me that life is worth working hard for."

MARY YEO

Mary Yeo, a teacher and camping saleswoman from Cumberland Center, Maine, was the only grandmother on the summit team. She had been diagnosed in 1989, at the age of fifty-three. Yeo was always active and always felt healthy. Even while she was awaiting the results of her biopsy she went hiking with a friend, saying, "You know, I don't think I have breast cancer. I feel so good." She had climbed Mount Kenya just a few months earlier. But the biopsy was positive; she had cancer in her right breast. Though it was an early case, pre-stage-one, she opted for a mastectomy.

One of Yeo's seven grown children was always with her during surgery and at doctor's appointments, and if she broke down would reassure her that everything was okay. "When diagnosed I thought it was a death sentence," she recalls. "Immediately I gathered all the information about breast cancer that I could find. Taking the situation one day at a time and with the wonderful support of my family, I got through surgery only to find that there is life after breast cancer." Two days before her surgery, her grandson Daniel—one of five grandchildren—was born.

Mary Yeo decided to climb Mount Aconcagua as a tribute to her five daughters, two sons, and husband for "their unfailing support of me during my time with breast cancer."

SUPPORT TEAMS

Support for the Summit Team was provided by guides Catie Casson, John Hanron, Heather MacDonald, Jeff Martin, Kurt Wedburg, and Peter Whittaker. Also lending support and aid were breast surgeon Bud Alpert, M.D.; JanSport's Paul Delorey; writer Andrea Gabbard; James Kay; Steve Marts; and Jeannie Morris.

Bud Alpert and Claudia Berryman-Shafer
make their way through thin air

CHAPTER ³
THE UPHILL BATTLE

THE STONE SENTINEL

With the climbers and funding in place, there was only one obstacle preventing Expedition Inspiration from reaching its goal—and this obstacle stood at 22,800 feet. On Friday, January 20, 1995, the eighteen-person Summit Team of Expedition Inspiration and its fifty-seven duffels of gear boarded Aerolinea Argentinas in Los Angeles for the thirteen-hour flight to Buenos Aires, Argentina. Five days later the Trek Team would follow.

Once settled in the town of Puenta del Inca, the team heard stories about how inclement weather had thwarted many climbers during the previous month. Other climbers told of a death on the mountain and many injuries.

Guide Peter Whittaker informed the EI climbers not to dwell on these events. "We are prepared for anything," he assured the team. To help the group acclimate and get rid of the jitters, Whittaker led them on a day hike several miles up and out of the valley to a ridge that opened up, giving the survivors their first real look at Aconcagua. They were all spellbound by the mountain. In the distance, Aconcagua—the Stone Sentinel—stood alone, an immense fortress of rock glazed with snow and ice. Like most of the world's highest peaks, it looked neither friendly nor inviting.

When Andrea Ravinett Martin later saw the mountain with the Trek Team, she burst into tears. "Everyone said that it was the ugliest of the world's seven highest peaks. But it was far from ugly. It was as massive as it was high, even from fifty miles away during a warm-up hike at the Horcone's trailhead. It sliced the sky at a majestic angle that seemed impossible to climb. I cried because of its beauty and because I had spent two years working for this. I cried remembering that six years ago to the day, a doctor had told me that I had little chance of surviving the next five years."

The plan for the climb was for the Summit Team to take the Polish Glacier Route on Aconcagua. This group would need to trek to two other camps, Las Lenas and Casa de Piedras, before even reaching the base camp, called Plaza Argentinas, located at 13,800 feet. The Summit Team would then continue on to Camp 1, located at 16,000 feet, then on to High Camp (Camp 2) at 19,000 feet, and from there they would attempt the summit climb. The Trek Team would be following days behind the first group, remaining at the base camp to lend support and prayers as the Summit Team ascended the mountain. Then, on Summit Day, many of the Trek Team would climb to over 15,000 feet to help the Summit Team descend with all their equipment.

Opposite: The summit team steps it up to the next level

An urban bagel lunch at 16,000 feet

"What started as a burden became a gift."

SARA HILDEBRAND

ONE DAY CLOSER FOR THE SUMMIT TEAM

On January 24, the Summit Team embarked on their long-awaited journey, starting at the trailhead for Las Vacas Valley. The path through the "Valley of the Cows" meandered up and down through the gorge of the Rio de Las Vacas, over loose rock and dusty scree. The trail was hard on the ankles and feet, especially at the quick pace that Whittaker had set to prepare the travelers for the climb to come. Five and a half hours and eight miles later, they reached Las Lenas and set up camp. It had been a good first day. Claudia Berryman-Shafer remarked, "We're one day closer to the summit."

Two days later the Summit Team reached base camp, where they climbed slowly so their bodies would have time to adjust to the altitude. They knew that if they ascended too quickly, they were at risk of getting altitude sickness and their adventure could be over in a heartbeat. Already the trekkers were feeling the effects of the altitude. They frequently ran out of energy and had to stop and take deep breaths.

Whittaker told the team that like cancer, the goal of mountaineering is to survive, to make a round trip of the adventure, adding, "Sometimes the survival involves the summit, and sometimes it doesn't." Likewise, sometimes your body will let you climb higher and other times it won't. Climbers must eat a high-calorie diet for fuel and drink plenty of water so they don't become dehydrated. Aside from altitude sickness, which can cause bouts of dizziness, headaches, and loss of energy, trekkers must be wary of chest congestion, which can lead to pulmonary edema (where the lungs fill with fluid that prevents breathing).

On Sunday, January 29, it took the Summit Team eight hours to carry half its gear and food from the 13,800-foot base camp to the 16,200-foot Camp 1, stow it there in stuff sacks anchored by large rocks, and return to base camp to sleep one more night. This would be the pattern for the rest of the climb, appropriately known as "carrying high and sleeping low." Though one of the Argentine rangers at base camp told Whittaker that a weather report from Chile forecast a storm during the next four days, the group decided to move on to Camp 1 the next day. Once on the mountain, every day counts, as a team can't carry enough extra food and supplies to make up for much lost time. If the group ran out of food or gas to heat the stove for melting snow for water, the climb would be over. Four hours later, all but two team members had reached Camp 1. Yeo had fallen behind, and guide Kurt Wedburg had stayed with her. Yeo recalls, "I had trouble coordinating pressure breathing and rest-stopping." These techniques are key to prevent burnout and be able to get adequate oxygen. She had also developed "climber cough," a dry, hacking cough that is a side effect of exertion at high altitude.

ONE DAY CLOSER FOR THE TREK TEAM

On January 31, the Trek Team finally started their own journey, following in the Summit Team's tracks. The winds were blowing at about fifty miles an hour. Duke, her limbs stiff from the chemo-induced rheumatoid arthritis, had a hard time keeping her footing in the wind's assault. She twisted her left leg in a fall, but recovered after about ten minutes. After the team reached Casa de Piedras, they received a radio transmission from the Summit Team, who were waiting out the blizzard at Camp 1. The teams took turns exchanging cheers to send each other energy. Then Whittaker radioed to say the Summit Team was going to carry on to Camp 2 the next day "no matter what the weather. This storm can't last." Later, the Trek Team had a sobering moment when they met two disoriented climbers who had summitted, but then abandoned all their gear in the storm in order to descend the mountain quickly. They had been lost, without food or shelter, for several days.

The next day, February 2, during the Trek Team's approach to base camp, Duke collapsed about an hour out. "I got a horrible headache, I felt numb from the knees down and tingly all over," she says. Dr. Ron Dorn and Ned Randolf stayed with her while guide Mark Tucker led the rest of the team to base camp. The three eventually joined the rest and were welcomed with cheers.

THE GOING GETS TOUGH

The following day the Summit Team radioed base camp to let them know that two climbers were coming back down. Guides Tucker and Olson were dispatched to escort them back to the base camp. That morning, the Summit Team began the climb to Camp 2, at 19,000 feet. As soon as they reached a snow-covered ridge at 17,500 feet, the wind whipped up again and began to knock the team around. Maintaining a steady pace was difficult. They'd take a few steps forward, then brace themselves as a gust hammered against their bodies and broke the tempo. Yeo knew from her experience the day before that she could not climb any higher. Writer Andrea Gabbard from the support team had developed congestion during the night and her face was swollen. They needed to turn back so they wouldn't jeopardize the team's success.

Without Yeo, only five breast cancer survivors remained on the Summit Team. Would the weather hold another two days and allow the team to reach the summit? Or would the mountain win this time?

Back at base camp, Tucker asked the Trek Team, "How many are interested in going to nineteen thousand feet tomorrow?" Several team members raised their hands, including Nancy Hudson, Nancy Johnson, Dr. Kathleen Grant, Dr. Ron Dorn, Sue Anne Foster, Claudia Crosetti, and Saskia Thiadens. The rest of the team would be on hand to help the Summit Team carry gear down if they needed assistance. Unfortunately, Thiadens

Paul Delorey and Laura Evans climb
uphill to descend from base camp

22,800 *feet*

The EI team trails along the base of
22,800 foot Mount Aconcagua

had a bad cold and a rattling cough. She was experiencing difficulty breathing and had a severe headache. Thiadens had to be evacuated from the camp to get medical attention for pulmonary edema. Two guides escorted her back down the mountain and to Mendoza to find a doctor.

By the time Thiadens and the guides had departed, it had grown too late to send a group of hikers up to nineteen thousand feet. Tucker had received a call from Whittaker alerting them that the Summit Team had left Camp 2 at five-thirty in the morning and had begun the ascent for the summit. Whittaker called again from 20,500 feet with mixed news. The good news was the weather was perfect for a summit; the bad news was that two more team members had turned around and were headed back to base camp with guides Wedburg and Casson. Several of the Trek Team members hiked up to 15,100 feet to intercept the descending climbers.

TOP OF THE WORLD

The best-laid plans of mountain climbers and breast cancer survivors often go awry. Summit Day broke cold but nearly windless and clear. Laura Evans was feeling the pressure. "I did not sleep well. I suspect nobody did," she recalled in her book. "At 19,000 feet, your heart races trying to compensate for the diminished oxygen in the air. Mine was racing for a different reason. Roger says I climb for validation that I am well, and of course he's right. I remembered when I could barely walk, my lungs so battered from cancer treatment. I had trained hard and knew that my limbs and determination would carry me up this mountain, further away from the hospital, further away from the crippling effects of the treatment, further from the mental anguish of the disease.

"At 23,000 feet, Aconcagua was higher than any of us had ever been. It was impossible not to wonder, what will it be like up there? What if I don't make it? So much was riding on this climb, highly publicized across the country, around the world. Everyone expected me to stand on the summit. What if. . . ."

That morning the Summit Team was getting ready for their big day when Paul Delorey announced that he wasn't going. He had developed sinus congestion that had worsened at high altitude. Delorey says, "I wanted to help the team get to the summit. I realized I might have put somebody else in jeopardy from going to the top. If it had only been me, I could have taken another day, rested up, and gone on. But it wasn't only me, it was the team."

The Summit Team, five remaining survivors and three guides, set off at 5:30 A.M. on February 4, 1995, roped together, the lights from their headlamps bobbing along the snowdrifts. Suddenly, Whittaker's light dropped. "Oh my god," Evans thought. Whatever had swallowed Whittaker would take her next. Suddenly, she was floundering in snow up to her chest. It was a scene repeated several times that morning. The snow was so deep in the upper reaches of Aconcagua that rock-hard, icy spires of it were buried in drifts. Every few steps, the team would flounder. Porter was in trouble. She pleaded for more rope as she began to slip behind. Within two hours, she would drop out, burying her face in the snow and sobbing.

Annette Porter had been determined to reach the summit, but eventually her body gave out. "I suddenly felt as if no air would go into my lungs," she recalls. Her leg from the knee down felt like wood, and her feet were icy. "I wanted to go to the top, but I guess it wasn't my day." Evans noted, "It was sad because Annette thought she was letting me down along with so many others, which wasn't true. There would be other summits for her. But it made me sad to see her sobbing, gasping for air, and to know that after all her hard work, this climb was over for her." Now there were only four breast cancer survivors in line for the summit.

Evans recorded a long, steep, relentless incline from Camp 2 to the point where the trail intersects with the Ruta Normal, an elevation gain of about fifteen hundred feet, all in new snow. The team climbed for three hours through darkness until they could take a break and sit "like lumps, barely moving" for close to a half hour. Vicki Boriak fell off pace and at the next break, around 21,500 feet, she and John Hanron were clearly far enough out that a decision had to be made. Boriak and Hanron turned back; another survivor was splitting off. It was another wrenching loss for the team that had endured so much together. That left three survivors: Nancy Knoble, Claudia Berryman-Shafer, and Laura Evans. With just two thousand feet to go, the team faced its toughest ascent yet. Now the survivors had to scramble up huge boulders. The jolting steps and jumps sent searing pains to Evans's injured "Rainier ankle." Heavy clouds hung overhead. But now they were close.

Meanwhile the Trek Team huddled around a walkie-talkie held by Peter Whittaker's wife, Erika. "Trek Team to Summit Team, are you there?" Erika asked. "We're fifteen feet from the summit," Whittaker finally answered. "We're going to make it!" Then, an interminable amount of time later, "Five minutes," he announced, panting. Then, at 4:00 P.M., he shouted: "We did it, you guys! We're on top!"

An overcome Roger Evans pulled the radio to himself. "We're so proud of you. This means so much," he said, his voice catching. "You've carried every one of our dreams up to that mountain and made them all come true. We love you. You couldn't have done anything in your lives more important than what you have just accomplished." "I'll tell you," his wife responded, laughing, "we busted our butts to make it!"

Evans had made her personal battle public with a dramatic top-of-the-world warrior cry against breast cancer. But the summit remained an intensely personal victory for her as well. She had fought back from the brink of death. She was proud of what her body had accomplished.

Elated summiteers Claudia Berryman-Shafer, Nancy Knoble, Laura Evans, and Peter Whittaker

"I've learned that you're not given a challenge in life without the wherewithal to get through it. It's just that sometimes you have to look really deep to find it."

ANNETTE PORTER

CHAPTER⁴

ECHOES FROM THE MOUNTAIN

The following morning, the team members in base camp mobilized to meet the Summit Team. A cadre of guides hit the trail to high camp before dawn to help the Summit Team carry down their gear. At eight-thirty, Nancy Johnson, Claudia Crosetti, Nancy Hudson, Ashley Sumner-Cox, Sue Anne Foster, Dr. Ron Dorn, Dr. Kathleen Grant, and Roger Evans took off with guide Jennifer Wedburg to intercept the descending climbers at Camp 1 and split up the load even further. Eleanor Davis, Roberta Fama, and Andrea Ravinett Martin climbed to 15,500 feet and waited there to greet the returning team. Those remaining at base camp prepared for the celebration party.

At three-thirty that afternoon, a long string of climbers appeared on the ridge above base camp. Everyone waved and cheered. One by one, the returning climbers made their way across the rocks into camp. From hospital to mountaintop, it had been a long journey to this moment of reunion. At last, sharing hugs, tears, and laughter, the team stood together again on the mountain.

The media coverage of Expedition Inspiration continued for several months. The PBS documentary premiered in the summer of 1995, and the entire team was honored at the White House, Congress, and the Supreme Court. Hillary Clinton introduced the team during her announcement of a new national mammogram program.

For Andrea Ravinett Martin and Laura Evans, the project had become a full-time job. Having raised over one million dollars through Expedition Inspiration, the duo agreed to part ways to allow each to pursue the promotion of breast cancer awareness and fund-raising according to her own vision. When asked how EI was able to meet its challenges, Martin says, "We all loved each other—that made all the difference."

Laura Evans died of a malignant brain tumor in 2000, but the legacy of what she started with Expedition Inspiration will resonate for lifetimes to come. For most of the team members, the climb became more than a metaphor for their breast cancer experience. The expedition had also established a foundation from which their lives would go forward, and forged a bond that remains unbroken to this day.

Ashley Sumner-Cox says, "I could hardly say the 'B' word . . . now I'll shout 'Breast!' at the top of my lungs. Being part of the team helped me find some peace and self-confidence. After I got back, I walked a little taller."

Opposite: Training day on Mount Rainer; (L—R) Nancy Knoble, Laura Evans, and Annette Porter

A victory for the Aconcagua climbers and The Breast Cancer Fund: Peter Whittaker, Laura Evans, Nancy Knoble, Bud Alpert, Claudia Berrymen-Shafer

Vicki Boriak now works helping medically underserved women in the Santa Clara County public health system with a group of "amazing people motivated by the heart, not the pocketbook." She also presents slide shows and talks about her experience on Aconcagua. "The thing I bring is fear," she says. "People see I'm young and fit and healthy. If I can get cancer, they realize anyone can."

"The climb was a healing journey," Kim O'Meara adds. "I'm a very different person now because of the cancer and because of the Aconcagua experience. I think I'm a better person. What I once thought was a horrible experience turned out to be a positive catalyst for change in my life."

Nancy Hudson concurs, saying, "EI gave me the opportunity to turn a horrifying experience into one of the most positive, valuable, and life-assuring events of my lifetime."

Sara Hildebrand shares a similar sentiment. "What started as a burden became a gift," she asserts. "I am a stronger person because of breast cancer and I have an obligation to help others with the disease as my climbing teammates helped me. I celebrate wellness every day as I continue to raise money for research and recovery programs for newly diagnosed women."

Looking back, Nancy Knoble says her best moment on the climb was rejoining the team at base camp. "Reaching the summit was wonderful, but being together on the mountain with the whole team was what I had looked forward to for a very long time," she says. "I really believe that a small group of committed people doing what they believe in can change the world. Yes, we were ordinary people doing the extraordinary, but you don't necessarily know that while you're doing it. It has to do with following your heart and following a passion and being committed."

Prayer flags set aloft on summit winds

"You can live with a life-threatening illness and
go on to achieve unlimited goals."

ANDREA GABBARD

Left: Climbers send their prayers of healing

Bottom: Together, climbers make their way across a spectacular landscape

PART 2

MOUNT MCKINLEY

CHAPTER⁵
THE NEXT STEP

+ **SURVIVORS TEAM**
Sandy Badillo
Mary Ann Castimore
Marcy Ely-Wilson
Nancy Knoble
Iris Lancaster

+ **PRINCETON TEAM**
Majka Burnhardt
Bethany Coates
Naomi Darling
Katie Gamble
Meg Smith

+ **HIGH ALTITUDE CLIMBERS**
Michele Potkin
Cathy Ann Taylor

+ **GUIDES/ PHOTOGRAPHERS**
Mimi Borquin
Tim Conkley
Lex Fletcher
Eli Helmuth
Alan Kearney
Marty Raney
Miles Raney
Michael Stilich
Julian Townsmeier

JOINING OF FORCES

After the success of Expedition Inspiration, Andrea Ravinett Martin knew that it was only the beginning. The next climb The Breast Cancer Fund would organize was slated for spring 1998 and would appropriately be known as "Climb Against the Odds." It would take place on 20,300-foot Mount McKinley, also known as Denali. Major funding had already been provided by North Face adventure gear, Volkswagen of America, and Lilith Fair concerts.

The McKinley climb was organized similarly to the Aconcagua trek, but with a crucial difference: The Summit Team would include five breast cancer survivors and a team of five women from Princeton University who had never had the disease, and two experienced high altitude climbers devoted to the issue. The groups were combined for a number of reasons, including to give the younger women a glimpse into their own increasingly possible futures, to inspire them, to inspire the older women, and to create an empathic link between survivors and the healthy, who might be able to translate the experience for those who remained blind to the runaway cancer toll.

Nobody said it would be easy. The McKinley expedition was a new challenge on several fronts for The Breast Cancer Fund after the organizers' first successful expedition to the top of Aconcagua. For one thing, the Denali Expedition numbered only twelve. It would be a lean and mean team on McKinley, versus the forty-two in Argentina, and all members would try to summit. There was to be no supporting trek team. In addition, weather would offer new obstacles. Not only would temperatures in Alaska be much colder, but severe, unpredictable changes in the weather make McKinley notoriously difficult to climb.

THE SURVIVORS

NANCY KNOBLE

Knoble was the obvious choice to head the team. Strong, personable, cool in the face of tension, she understood the importance of The Breast Cancer Fund climbs to both the public and the participants. The Aconcagua summit had changed her life—even more so than breast cancer. "A number of people have asked me how breast cancer changed my life. I don't know that it was really my diagnosis that was a turning point for me," Knoble says. "For me, it was the Aconcagua expedition, which happened a year after my graduation

Opposite: The Climb Against the Odds McKinley Team

from radiation. That was the first time since my diagnosis that I had a big chunk of time when I could be really reflective and really think about myself. I spent sixteen days on that mountain, hiking along, carrying my packs. No telephone, no pager, no fax machine. That was the time when I really started to stack up my priorities and say: How am I living life? How do I want to live it differently?"

After Expedition Inspiration, in 1997, Knoble had a new primary diagnosis, stage-one invasive cancer, for which she had a bilateral mastectomy. After Aconcagua, she also quit being a desk jockey in corporate America to volunteer, to have time for herself, and to continue climbing mountains.

Knoble believed the main priority of the McKinley climb was that the survivors and Princeton women move up the mountain together. "I personally don't want to summit without them," said Knoble. She believed the climb had to demonstrate a link between victims of a disease and the rest of the world. Her goal on Mount McKinley was to "get as high as we can in a positive way, [conveying the] real message that we're not going to lick this problem alone. The reason for being here is the experience of being on the mountain together. Reaching the summit is secondary. It's not enough for breast cancer survivors to climb this mountain alone. . . . A bigger part of the power in the fight against breast cancer is with those who don't have the disease, but who understand the issue. We don't stand a chance of beating breast cancer unless we can ignite the energy of young women who haven't had breast cancer to get out there and take good care of themselves, to raise funds, to raise awareness."

SANDY BADILLO

Sandy Badillo, a mother of three and grandmother of five, had been diagnosed with breast cancer in 1990. She was playing pro tennis at the time, backpacking regularly, kayaking, and windsurfing. She had just escorted a group of junior tennis players on the national circuit in New York and returned home with what felt like a case of the flu. After a battery of tests, her doctor told her "You're the healthiest patient I have." But there was still one test to go—a mammogram. It revealed a small white lump, what Badillo recalls looked like "a comet surrounded by the Milky Way." It was the spiraling white galaxy that particularly concerned her doctor. The sprinkles of dots were microcalcifications, a common indication of breast cancer. A biopsy confirmed their suspicions.

What followed was a brutal regime common to thousands of breast cancer survivors. Badillo lost her left breast, then underwent nine months of chemotherapy and six weeks of radiation. Even with that rigorous treatment, her doctor gave her only a 30 percent chance of surviving the next two years.

Yet eight years later, Badillo was challenging a mountain too daunting for many veteran climbers. Climbing Denali was important to her to raise awareness about breast

Sandy Badillo suited up, sanguine, and ready to go

14,000 *fee*

Mount Shasta was a stepping stone to
Denali for Sandy Badillo

cancer, but also because it was crucial to her personal struggle against her disease. Somehow the climb had become inexorably connected to Badillo's cancer battle, a battle she views as one primarily of the will. She believed that if she could face down fear, she could conquer her disease. Training climbs on Mount Shasta to prepare for Denali sometimes scared Badillo out of her wits. "The thought, the negative thought, comes into mind how dangerous this really is," she says. "I could be hurt. But then, that positive voice will take over and push me further."

If anyone was the team cheerleader, it was Badillo, who was the one most likely to burst into song or tell a joke. She was convinced her cancer was beat, and she would storm this mountain. "I never do anything halfway," she says. "When I really believe in something, or think I can really do it, I go for it. Maybe I'm a little naïve about it. But I'm not out there trying to climb the seven tallest peaks in the world. I'm thinking, just one mountain."

On her way to a training climb aboard a small prop plane, Badillo mentioned to the pilot that she was going to climb Denali. "You?" he asked incredulously. "I think you should seriously consider this a little more. This is a serious mountain. You just don't put on your backpack and take off." She explained she was climbing to raise awareness about breast cancer. "He said to me, 'I think you're taking the climb a little too lightly,'" Badillo recalled. "I told him, 'I think you're taking breast cancer a little too lightly.'"

It wasn't just the climb that had hooked Badillo. She was desperate for a Denali summit. She believed the best place for the climbers to take a stand to fight breast cancer was from the very top of the highest peak of the continent. She explained, "What we're really looking at here is the breast cancer survivors' need to summit, to make it realistic and make the climb accomplish the goals we're all here to accomplish."

MARY ANN CASTIMORE

Three years before the climb, Mary Ann Castimore awoke one morning with a bad pain in her chest. It turned out to be a fracture caused by a malignant tumor in her sternum— metastasized cancer from her original stage-one breast cancer diagnosis almost ten years earlier. "Doctors were totally amazed that it had come back, and come back with such a vengeance," she says. "That was a real tough time. It's incurable, inoperable."

The forty-one-year-old Christmas-tree farmer from Augusta, New Jersey, was a walking advertisement that the devastating disease can reside in the breasts of even those who appear to be glowing with good health. She was particularly apprehensive about climbing with an active case of breast cancer.

While training, Castimore worried that she wouldn't measure up for the Denali challenge. Her biggest fear was "having such a heavy load and not being able to keep up. That's not what I'm going there for. I'm not going to give up." To get in shape for the

67
MOUNT MCKINLEY

Left: Marcy Ely-Wilson rappels the face of a rock during the Sierra training climb

Bottom: Shakedown climbers practice summit victories for Climb Against the Odds McKinley Top (L–R): Alan Kearney and Nancy Knoble Bottom (L–R): Iris Lancaster, Marcy Ely-Wilson, Janet Calmels, and Sandy Badillo

hike, Castimore routinely walked a treadmill carrying a backpack with sixty-five-pound weights. On training climbs, her strategy was to succeed one careful step at a time. "You don't look down and say, 'I'm taking this step, this step. . . . ' You do your power steps and you do your power breathing. If it gets real bad, I start counting steps. If I get to a hundred, I look up and say, 'Gee, I'm a lot further than I was before.'" Castimore imagined herself on the summit countless times: "The picture in my head is I'm totally exhausted, more than probably bursting into tears . . . and I'm going to fall on my knees and thank God for getting me there."

+ An emotional day at Anchorage Race for Cancer;
Marcy Ely-Wilson and Sandy Badillo

MARCY ELY-WILSON

Marcy Ely-Wilson, a fifty-year-old teacher and therapist from Napa, California, was diagnosed in 1991 with a .5-centimeter tumor in her right breast. She underwent a modified radical mastectomy, including lymph nodes. Her cancer was stage-one and she received tamoxifen for five years, at which point she was declared a statistical cure. Then, in 1997, Ely-Wilson was diagnosed with a recurrence of her breast cancer, which metastasized to her liver. She underwent chemotherapy followed by stem-cell replacement therapy.

When Ely-Wilson saw the climb video of Aconcagua, she was frustrated that she had not known about it early enough to participate. Within a few weeks of viewing the video, she saw the announcement for the Mount McKinley climb and immediately responded. "I really wanted to climb Mount McKinley on behalf of other women facing the disease," she said.

The 1997 recurrence of her breast cancer only intensified Ely-Wilson's resolve to climb Mount McKinley. The metaphor of climbing and beating cancer became a focus, giving her purpose and motivation to continue the fight. She saw her struggle with the disease as a mountaineer views the battle with a peak: "I get down in a crevasse again. It's a deep crevasse. It's cold. It's terrible. I've fallen. I'm scared. I could die down there. And if I lie there I will."

In a training climb on Mount Baker, fellow climber Iris Lancaster described Ely-Wilson as a woman who "swore like a sailor and climbed like a mountain goat, [and] was the voice and strength behind our climb. She never left you wondering about what she was thinking. When Marcy had a passion it

permeated her being and she could not sit silently. Climbing Mount McKinley for The Breast Cancer Fund became one of her greatest passions. When the project sputtered, her passion fueled it, keeping our dreams to climb alive. That same determined resolve seemed to spill onto those lucky enough to be around Marcy."

The McKinley Team members race in Anchorage to raise awareness of the climb

IRIS LANCASTER

Iris Lancaster, a teaching consultant for learning-disabled children in Michigan, was diagnosed with breast cancer just days before her thirty-eighth birthday. She had a tender, swollen area under her left arm. The swelling was cyclical and harmless, but a mammogram showed a growth on her right side—something she would not have otherwise detected. For Lancaster, who had a mastectomy, the diagnosis was like a recurring nightmare. "I've lost some family members and friends to cancer," she says. "If you can think of something disintegrating or falling in a pile on the floor, that's how I felt when I got the diagnosis on the phone. I threw myself on the bed. I fell apart. I literally fell apart for days."

But it wasn't long before Lancaster decided she had to make something positive of the experience: "From the very beginning, I wanted this to be more than just me having had breast cancer. I wanted it to be bigger than that. I've always been involved in the outdoors and this climb was a natural way to go. I don't know who wrote this, but it goes something like: 'I'd rather be ashes than dust, a meteor than a star, a flash across the

The McKinley Team at Lilith Fair

sky in one fleeting moment of glory than remain sedentary the rest of my life. . . . ' All of us are trying to make something positive happen out of a negative experience."

Training was a transforming experience for Lancaster, who considered herself in better shape at the start of the expedition than at any other time in her life. That fact alone gave hope to a woman who had believed she was destined to die an early death from breast cancer, as so many before her have. "My grandmother's name was Rose, my mother's name was Lily, and I'm Iris," she says. "We came from this line of flowers. My grandmother died at fifty-eight, my mother at fifty-four, so I figured the natural progression would be fifty for me. But now I'm more hopeful. The closer I get to fifty, the more I think that's probably not going to happen."

THE PRINCETON TEAM

Strength is a relative thing, and the young women who would climb McKinley alongside the survivors would discover the true meaning of the word. The five members of the Princeton team, Majka Burnhardt, Bethany Coates, Naomi Darling, Katie Gamble, and Meg Smith, were students at the university. They all had climbing experience, but had attempted nothing like Mount McKinley. These women would experience more than another challenging summit attempt. After training for over a year, they would learn the kind of survival skills not taught in mountaineering school—from women who have faced breast cancer.

Besides the Princeton crew, the team would include experienced high-altitude climbers—Alaskan climber Michele Potkin and Cathy Ann Taylor, a Himalayan guide with Mountain Travel Sobek. Michael Stilich, Julian Townsmeier, and Tim Connley would join Eli Helmuth and Mimi Borquin to guide the team. Miles Raney, Marty Raney, Alan Kearney, and Lex Fletcher were also on hand to document the experience.

Katie Gamble, Naomi Darling, and Meg Smith in excellent spirits after conquering Denali.

CHAPTER 6

A ROUGH START

THE "ALIEN" RETURNS

In a dramatic change of fortune that would be aired nationwide on ABC television's *20/20*, Marcy Ely-Wilson's expedition plans came to a crashing halt just weeks before the start of the climb. Her breast cancer, first diagnosed in 1991, had come raging back in her liver a year before the expedition. Again, she had attacked her disease with radiation and full stem-cell destruction. But one month before the McKinley climb was to begin, she discovered that the cancer had metastasized to her brain.

Ely-Wilson's husband, Charley, recalls the day he and his wife discovered the grim news with cameras rolling: "There is a macabre sense of what was going on there. We actually allowed the crew to go in there and film the CAT scan procedure. Then we were sitting there waiting for the radiologist to read the report. He was in the room with us and we were all watching [the images] come up on the screen. [Suddenly], he freaks out, asks everyone to leave, and says he is not going to discuss this case on camera."

Ely-Wilson was the survivor climber closest to the monster. She described her cancer as "the alien. That's the thing I didn't ask for and nobody in my family or my peer group asked for it. It's bad and you can't make deals with it." She was crushed by the devastating news, but was determined to join the team at base camp in Alaska to show her support.

THE DANGERS OF DENALI

Uncertainties added to growing tensions in Talkeetna, Alaska, while the group waited impatiently for a window of good weather and their turn on the plane headed to the glacier at Denali's base. Days dragged on in the town, a dreary strip of road resembling Cicely on the television show *Northern Exposure*. Used to only a few women hitting Denali's flanks (only 7 percent of the climbers have been female), the locals had already begun to speak derisively of the breast cancer expedition, referring to the women in their matching yellow North Face climbing clothes as the "Yellow Bees" and the "Chiquitas."

Guide Eli Helmuth welcomed the women at the start of the expedition with a warning about Denali's "terrible beauty" and "violence." The climb, he emphasized, would be "the most work we've ever done in our lives." He prepared the climbers for the very real possibility that they would not summit. He says, "To me, making the summit is

Opposite: The Princeton Team happily adjusts to the cold

A stunning aerial view of Mount McKinley

"McKinley is a walk in the park; cancer is the big mountain."

MARCY ELY-WILSON 1948–1999

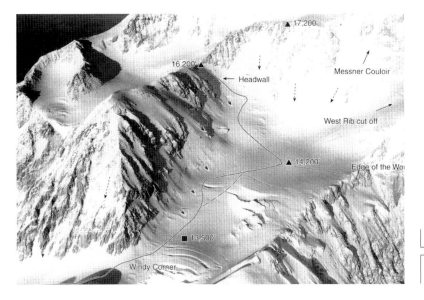

16,200'▲
▲ 17,200'
← Headwall
Messner Couloir
West Rib cut off
▲ 14,200'
Edge of the Wo
■ 13,500'
Windy Corner

The McKinley route map

the frosting on the cake. The cake is the climb. Our biggest concern as guides is safety. We know we'll have had a successful expedition when everyone returns without frostbite, injury, or illness."

It was a particularly extreme year on the mercurial mountain. The top reaches of Denali are compared to the Death Zone of Everest, where the thin air wastes bodies and debilitates minds, sapping a climber's will not only to summit, but to eat, to drink, and even to live. But weather conditions in 1998, on the heels of El Niño, made this an exceptionally mean season for climbers. Winds could reach a high velocity on the mountain's higher reaches. One mountain guide said that "if you squat to tie your boot laces, you risk losing your balance and finding yourself at the bottom of a crevasse."

Just weeks into the climbing season, the harsh weather had already claimed the lives of three climbers who were blown or fell off Denali's windy West Buttress. One of them, a guide, was buffeted off his feet to his death as Helmuth, who was leading another expedition nearby, watched helplessly.

There had been no successful summits in May. So far, only a third of McKinley climbers were making it to the top. Usually about half succeeded. Though eleven hundred climbers had obtained permits to try for the top, only three hundred had shown up to actually make a bid.

The guides carefully explained to the breast cancer group, again, the risks the climbers face when they push their bodies above sixteen thousand feet, where the blood can no longer easily adjust to the reduced level of oxygen in the air. At this height, where there is about half the amount of oxygen as at sea level, the body's functions are significantly impaired. Everything takes longer, as the brain struggles with hypoxia. The simplest things, like melting snow for water, can become a tremendous test of the will. The lack of oxygen can turn deadly fast. The most serious problem is cerebral edema, when the brain swells and climbers can quickly slip into a coma.

Lungs are another particularly vulnerable organ, susceptible on the mountain to pulmonary edema, in which the body is drowning from the inside out. Guide Mimi Borquin explains, "It's fluid accumulating in your lungs. You cannot keep living with pulmonary edema." The climbers were told that if any of them got it, the climb would be over and they would be going back down. Even on days when their lives weren't threatened, Borquin warned the climbers that they would likely suffer acute mountain sickness: "You won't feel good. At some point on the mountain you'll just wake up in the morning and feel like you've got a really bad hangover."

But the climbers were optimistic. The breast cancer survivors who had experienced chemotherapy knew what it was like to wake up in the morning feeling like death. "Breast cancer was the challenge. McKinley will be a walk in the park," scoffed fifty-two-year-old Sandy Badillo, quoting one of Ely-Wilson's favorite lines.

THE SPLIT

+ Katie Gamble and Majka Burnhardt relax in Talkeetna after the climb

Another blow came to the team when the park services ruled the group was too large to move safely up the mountain as a single entity and had to split into two. Calmly, in a large lodge room of the Park Services building in Talkeetna, Knoble expressed her views and solicited ideas from the rest of the team. Once on the mountain, if the weather was right, should the first group wait for the second so that the two teams could ascend together, or should they go separately? The Princeton women, guides, and survivors sprawled on the floor and furniture alongside the cameramen, who included mountain moose Marty Raney and assistant Miles Raney, cancer survivor Lex Fletcher, and wry still photographer Alan Kearney.

Knoble explained she wanted the two groups to ascend at the same pace. She hoped if the groups became separated, one would wait for the other so they could continue together, "even if it does compromise the goal of getting to the summit." Like survivor Sandy Badillo, most of the Princeton women were clearly hungry for a summit by somebody on the team and wanted the team's eye on the prize. This would be the first real test of Knoble's leadership. It would largely be up to her to reconcile the individual drive that can contribute to the success of a mountaineering expedition with the message of concern and the unity that was the mission of the climb.

ABC interviews survivors in Talkeetna, Alaska;
Bottom (L–R): Nancy Knoble and Iris Lancaster.
Top (L–R): Mary Ann Castimore, Marcy Ely-Wilson,
and Sandy Badillo

"I climbed for my daughters, my sisters, my family,
and my friends and for all the women of the world."

SANDY BADILLO

Katie Gamble breaks for a cold drink
on Kahiltna Glacier

Princeton climber Katie Gamble pointed out, "You have to take the windows. If you're flying first to the glacier and the weather opens up, go for it." Guide Helmuth similarly warned, "The way the weather has been going this month, the trend has been one that continues to work against big groups and works for the groups that move whenever they can. A style focused on staying together is not a style that's going to get us to the summit." He emphasized that in any case, a smaller group is safer and more efficient, using the example of eighteen climbers waiting in the frigid air for a couple of teammates to tie their boots: "It's the kind of occurrence likely repeated several times a day which can quickly kill an expedition's momentum."

The team finally reached a consensus that the Princeton students would make up one group and the survivors the other, with the aim that the teams would rendezvous at camps whenever reasonable. The lineup would be reassessed at fourteen thousand feet before the last big push to the summit. Ultimately though, the mountain would decide.

It was left to Princeton student Meg Smith and survivor Marcy Ely-Wilson to dissolve the stress caused by the division. "Despite the split we are still one team," said Smith, whose great-grandmother, great-aunt, and mother are all breast cancer survivors. "If Nancy stands on the summit and I don't, I'm still a pretty satisfied climber. I don't like the idea of people waiting. If I'm on the team behind, I want the team to go. Anyone standing on the summit is a victory for everyone in this room. If there are two people on the summit, they carry everyone's spirit there. If I'm one of them, I'm psyched. If I'm not one of them, I'm still psyched."

Ely-Wilson, the woman who had been most like a mother to the team, told the climbers that despite their position on the mountain, the teams would always be together in spirit, just as she would be with them at heart. Of Ely-Wilson, Gamble said, "Before me sat a woman who was obviously dying, yet ran ten miles a few days ago and is here in Alaska to send us off. Marcy is an inspiration to me and to the whole group. There is a chance that we will never see her again after today. At one point, I climbed for myself. Now I climb for them." Ely-Wilson was supposed to be climbing now with the survivors. Instead she was restlessly shifting in her chair, her fingers touching the sky-blue kerchief over the radiation burns on her head.

By heart would be the only way Ely-Wilson would join the climb. Though she ached to at least reach base camp with them, she would never leave Talkeetna. A wave of exhaustion and a troubling rash would keep her from her dream.

As the tearful climbers huddled around Ely-Wilson before taking off for the glacier, this inspirational woman told them: "Marcy has to take care of Marcy. You have to climb for yourselves and others. If you love me, love yourselves. Take care every minute you're on that mountain." Marcy Ely-Wilson wouldn't live to see another spring.

CHAPTER 7
MEET THE MOUNTAIN

THE SMELL OF SUCCESS

The approach to Denali is zigzagged with dark hillocks, jagged pines, and ribbons of snow. The immensity of the terrain was abundantly clear to the climbers as they huddled in the seats of a red Cessna. The plane seemed to hover in the air forever before it made any headway from one stretch of landscape to another. It was the last time in weeks the climbers would see anything green, and it was the last time they'd be warm and dry for more than a few hours at a time.

As the plane's whining engine threatened to sabotage attempts at conversation, survivor Iris Lancaster recalled a recent dream: "I dreamed that I traveled to Russia to play the reigning world chess champion in a tournament. But when I arrived I found the rules had changed. Besides the fact that nobody spoke English, all my chess pieces looked like pawns. I knew my dream was about the climb. When I first laid eyes on Denali, it was clear we would be playing this game on her terms. Only a fool would say they could beat this mountain. In fact, many believe only a fool would try."

The survivors were excited but apprehensive. Though they had trained carefully for the climb, this would be the first big test of their post-cancer bodies. Arrival at the base camp at 7,200 feet on the Kahiltna glacier at the base of Denali did little to allay anyone's concerns. The plane was swarmed by ragged climbers with desperate faces. "It was surreal," says Lancaster. The climbers, from various expeditions, had been pinned down for five days by the weather, waiting for planes that couldn't fly in to get them back to Talkeetna. But as quickly as the weather would allow the plane to ferry in The Breast Cancer Fund team, it would close in again, stranding the pilot with part of the team for twenty-four hours.

The landscape quickly turned bleak. Denali's peak was completely veiled by a close wall of white, with low clouds and snow smudging the horizon. Visibility was a mere fifty yards. The temperature hovered a few degrees above zero; twenty-mile-per-hour winds whipped intermittent snowflakes against the climbers' exposed cheeks.

"It was like landing on the moon," said Sandy Badillo. But Lancaster was grateful that visibility was so poor. "I didn't want to see the peak," she recalls. "I didn't want to see how far we had to go."

The climbers slogged in snow up to their knees to quickly establish camp in the few short hours before midnight, when the bright Alaskan sky would fade to twilight.

Opposite: Sound-hearted Naomi Darling on Heartbreak Hill

"Surround my body
 You greatly powerful women
 Enlighten my soul."

CATHY ANN TAYLOR

Nancy Knoble and Sandy Badillo
muscle the supplies off the plane
at basecamp

8,000 feet

+ A view of the living room

Snow shelters had to be dug out to protect the tents from the wind, snow trampled to create a level surface, tents erected, prayer flags mounted, gear unpacked or stowed, and a site dug out for the kitchen, with snow benches and shelves for the portable stoves.

Melting snow for water is a mammoth task for climbers. Team members had to spend up to seven hours doing this, as it's easy to become dehydrated in the dry air of the mountain and vitally important to drink fluids. Guide Julian Townsmeier says he frequently drank five quarts a day on Denali, seven if he could get it. Of course, when you drink a lot, you also need to urinate a lot. The women came prepared: they brought pee funnels so they could perform this function with minimal skin exposure to the freezing elements.

The first strenuous night, the climbers fell exhausted into chilly sleeping bags in their three-person tents. It was a taste of things to come. "Hard labor" would be the operative phrase. The climbers had no sherpas or yaks to transport their tons of equipment up the hill. Each climber had to haul seventy to ninety pounds of equipment—some on her back, the rest towed on sleds. The equipment included personal items, clothing, hundreds of pounds of high-calorie food, pots, pans, utensils, and innumerable bottles of fuel for stoves.

Five different camps were established from bottom to top. Each camp was established in two stages, with climbers hauling up some supplies, burying them in a snow cache, retreating for a day to the previous camp, then hauling up what remained.

Climbing would be interrupted by days of unplanned rest as climbers waited for the weather to improve and for their bodies to acclimate to higher altitudes. At a certain point, even resting becomes difficult at too high an altitude.

Top: Cathy Ann Taylor and Nancy Knoble share the network in the tent on Kahiltna Glacier

Right top: The Climb Against the Odds film crew and set-up

Right bottom: A serene camp of prayer flags

Top: Climbers gain ground on the chaste
Windy Corner

Left: A frozen frame of Cathy Ann Taylor,
Michele Potkin, and Nancy Knoble

The first day's trek, from base camp to the second camp at 8,000 feet, was arduous for the survivors. A lengthy struggle with equipment ensued as they adjusted straps, tied down packs, and organized and reorganized loads. With three women in a tent, each wearing several pairs of socks and mittens, and with water bottles everywhere, "it takes a long time to find everything," says Lancaster. The survivors would make it to camp in five hours of hiking, the Princeton women in three.

The second day, the team moved out more quickly as familiarity with equipment and routine made the women more efficient. At the end of the day, a sunburned Badillo had enough energy to attack her chore of digging out a new kitchen with vigor. She declared the day's progress "fantastic, definitely better than yesterday," adding, "Yesterday, I was kind of lagging. There was too much heat on my body, not enough water in my system. Today was different. We kicked ice." Mary Ann Castimore was tired but strong as she prepared the evening meal of rice, chicken, and spices, or "Chef's Surprise," as she called it. Mimi Borquin, who had trained the women from the start over a two-year period, declared the day "okay, but not great," because she was sick. She reassured everyone that she simply had a cold, and not altitude sickness. The women were doing very well, much better than Borquin had first anticipated they would.

The climbers would get into the routine, easing the rough spots. The Princeton women, while all strong and moving quickly, still found the mountain demanding more. "Yesterday was a long day, moving up from 8,000 feet. I was exhausted," wrote Darling. "I just wanted to crawl into my sleeping bag and go to sleep. Instead, we kept climbing higher and higher. When you're on a rope team you can't just stop whenever you want. The others on the rope team keep pushing you on. Like running with other people, everyone pushes themselves individually, but everyone is also pushed by the team."

Mary Ann Castimore and Nancy Knoble were upbeat and tough. Badillo and Lancaster were struggling, but hanging in. "That was no walk in the park," Lancaster groaned at the end of one particularly grueling day. The conditions gradually became tougher, the slopes steeper, the temperatures lower, the wind faster. The climbers filled their sleeping bags with things they didn't want to freeze. They commonly stuffed cold, soggy socks in their armpits or over their hearts to dry them before morning. "It's been blowin' and snowin,'" Knoble said at ten thousand feet. At twenty below zero, "you have to sleep with your water, your cold water bottle, to keep it from freezing. You're surrounded by wetness. Everything is damp and soggy and cold."

The day the women climbed Motorcycle Hill was both one of their worst days and one of their best. Motorcycle Hill was the steepest slope of the climb they had encountered so far. It tops out at Windy Corner, where winds can reach seventy miles per hour. Lancaster recalls of that night, "I had a terrible night's sleep. It had nothing to do with altitude. I didn't have a headache. It [was] just the anticipation of the [next] climb

Top left: Campers gather around
the table in the kitchen

Top right: At the end of the day;
Sandy Badillo retires to her tent

and hoping I could do it. It's the big test." Knoble wondered, "We're being pushed to our limit, but can we do it?"

The women, tethered to one another by lines, snaked up the slopes, resting as a group, with some breaks between each step. The day was an endless series of hard, heavy breaths, labored footsteps in crunching snow, and screaming muscles. As they neared the top, Badillo called out, "Come on! Remember why we're doing this. Let's do it for Marcy!"

Sometimes the toughest days turn out to be among some of the most rewarding. For the first time during the expedition, the sun shattered the clouds while the Princeton team was descending from a carry to 10,000 feet back down to 8,000. "For the first time we stopped and looked around and really saw where we were," says Meg Smith. "From there we practically skipped down." The women headed for a cul-de-sac at 8,000 feet, stripped their tops down to sports bras, and danced. The rest of the team rested, laughed, and watched the face of Mount Foraker slough off a series of avalanches in the heat; it was close enough to be thrilling, yet far enough to do them no harm. In the crisp thin air, Denali's vivid peak seemed a mere arm's length away. "This is why we came to Alaska, this is why we climb," said Smith.

At ten thousand feet, the survivors had their own day to dance on Denali in the sunshine. A Spanish climber from another expedition sang them the only English words he knew—the lyrics to a rock song, "Fire." Badillo, sweaty blonde hair clinging to her cheeks, stripped to her white long underwear top and swung some provocative moves. "Let's dance, girls!" she said. On the best day, in the clear air, on top of the world, the sky was stark raving blue and the climbers could see the curve of the earth below. "There is no place in the world I'd rather be," was Knoble's way to describe it. Unfortunately, the rest of the climb would not be quite so picture perfect.

11,000 *feet*

Hikers not bikers on Motorcycle Hill

+ Squirrel Hill in all her glory

12,000 *feet*

The team hugs Nancy Knoble before she descends back to the base

THE AGONY OF DEFEAT

Guide Mimi Borquin had said she was sick. Meg Smith couldn't hold down her food, but thought the cause was bad bread at first. Ultimately, the biggest obstacle of the climb wasn't the mountain itself; it was much, much smaller: a virus. But when the trouble started, it built as quickly as an avalanche.

Everyone coughs on the mountain. Everyone has some kind of altitude sickness at one time or another. It becomes dangerous only when the cough turns into pulmonary edema, or becomes so serious that it jeopardizes a climber's strength. The team soon realized that the increasing chorus of coughs was something more than a normal mountain hack. Teammates joked that their mission had changed from "Climb Against the Odds" to "Climb Against the Flu." But everyone quit laughing at 11,000 feet. "I'm going down. Sickness has invaded our camp. It's time to go. It's not worth risking health for a mountain," announced Borquin. "But they'll make it. They'll make everyone happy and proud. There is no doubt in my mind that they're going to make it." Cameraman Marty Raney also headed back. "I never get sick, but I'm sick now," he said. "Sometimes you come here and you ace the mountain and other times, it humbles you."

By the next morning, Smith, Lancaster, and Badillo had joined them. Badillo woke early to pack and prepare for the next ascent, but she couldn't keep her oatmeal down. Smith, who only the day before had been reveling in her hardened body, woke with a "head like cement" and knew she was sick. It was a bitter pill to swallow. One of the self-described "animal women" who climbed fast and hard had fallen and felt betrayed by her body, an experience the survivors know so well. "You try to push as hard as [you can] . . . and suddenly your body is your enemy," Smith says.

As the team was reeling from the loss of five members, they had one more sobering reminder of the power of the mountain. Guides from the team helped with two major rescues: of a Japanese climber and the Spanish climber who had sung to the women. Both were suffering from pulmonary edema and had to be carried to medical help. The measure of oxygen in the Spaniard's system registered 37 percent on an oximeter; a normal reading is close to 85 percent. "That's pretty much circling the toilet bowl," said guide Julian Townsmeier, who helped carry the climber to the medical tent. "He could have died easily."

At 13,000 feet, the team found themselves at Windy Corner, known for having deadly winds. Princeton climber Katie Gamble remembers her frozen fingers of one hand clasping a fixed rope, while the other clung to an ice pick hooked into the mountain's flank. She balanced on her toes and jabbed into the wall with the crampons strapped to her hiking boots. Beneath her yawned a quarter-mile plunge; around her roiled snow, driven thicker and more furious by a rising wind. Head guide Eli Helmuth was a blur of

Right: Marty Raney serenades the team

Bottom: The last fatiguing day on Heartbreak Hill

red and yellow some hundred yards beneath her. Above her, teammate Bethany Coates clung to her piece of icy rock and faced her own demons as the winds revved to forty-five miles per hour. Miniature snowdrifts filled the insides of Gamble's glacier glasses, blocking her vision. "I went by feeling and kept telling myself that if blind people had climbed McKinley, so could I," she recalls.

Gamble was breathing hard, one forceful exhale for every two strong intakes of breath, to draw as much oxygen as she could from the thin air. She had an extra pair of gloves in her backpack, but couldn't let go of the rope for an instant to get them. Gamble worried that she would lose her fingers to the cold. Days earlier she had watched a U.S. Park Services film on McKinley hazards that was required viewing for all climbers. She recalled the disturbing pictures of black fingers and toes, reminding climbers to bring an extra pair of socks. At the time, she had written optimistically in her journal: "I have four pairs of socks and vapor booties . . . as for my hands, I have two pairs of liners and these big modular mitts. That should be warm enough!"

Now she wasn't so sure. Gamble wiggled the fingers of one hand in a fruitless attempt to get some modicum of feeling back. She felt queasy; she knew in the worst-case scenario, losing her fingers might be the best that could happen to her. Corpses had already been carried off the mountain that season. As Gamble climbed, two British soldiers, both experienced climbers, were stranded somewhere near the summit. Days earlier, lounging in the sun, she had spotted one of them huddled on a ledge at 19,000 thousand feet. For Gamble, what had been planned as a simple supply transport from one mountain camp to another had become what she would later describe in her journal as "too damn vicious."

Still the team pressed on, attacking the headwall to 16,500 feet, where they cached supplies for three days. It was the most demanding and most technical section of the climb, and required climbers to ascend a rocky wall clinging to fixed ropes. Michele Potkin labeled the day's climb a "humbling" experience, but she, Knoble, and Castimore negotiated well. The Princeton women followed the survivors up the fixed lines and descended into the teeth of a storm. It so badly frightened Princeton leader Gamble that she set a series of conditions for herself before she would take another step on Denali. "I will not go to high camp unless it is a perfect day, I will not go unless I am feeling perfect. I will not let my team go unless they are feeling perfect," were her vows.

Gamble forgot all the reasons she had come: to publicize breast cancer, to revel in her strength, to conquer a challenge. At that instant, she realized with the same clarity that Marcy Ely-Wilson discovered the first day of diagnosis that the thing that mattered most was living. She recalls: "I thought about Maine, my family, my house, my friends, love, sailing, sun . . . all of the things in life that make it worthwhile. It was like looking death in the eye. So now I wonder, what am I doing here? The point, after all, is to live."

14,000 feet

+ A cold but flat stretch on the mountain

If Gamble was hoping for reassurance that Denali was not dangerous, it wasn't coming soon. Four climbers, two Americans and two Brits, fell off the windy West Rib. The Americans fell 2,000 feet, the fall leaving one in critical condition, the other "beat up," according to a ranger. "I was just getting ready to go to bed and I looked out the door of the tent and I saw the British climbers both slide down about 1,000 feet and over the Bergshrund and come to a stop," recalls Les Lloyd, a guide from another expedition. "One of them was relatively uninjured. We watched him stagger down, trying to make it to the ranger station, and we watched him fall into a crevasse and basically disappear from sight." Meanwhile, the two other British climbers were still stranded at 19,000 feet. "Things aren't looking good for those guys," said a Denali ranger. "I am not very hopeful at this point."

The team doggedly continued to push for the summit. The plan would be to rest a day, then do a second carry to 17,000 feet. Three days of supplies would be cached there, so climbers could wait for the weather to relent before climbing to the top. If they ran out of food, they could head back to 16,000 feet to retrieve the supplies needed. The Princeton women spent a long afternoon in the kitchen, reorganizing food packages for the final ascent. One bag with special food had been labeled in big red letters, "Summit Day." Nearby in their tent, Townsmeier and photographer Alan Kearney listened to a ranger's weather predictions, learning they would most likely be socked in for three days. Kearney joked with Townsmeier, making cracks about his pee bottle. Only hours later, Kearney was seriously ill with pulmonary edema and needed to descend. He was rushed to the medical tent in the middle of the night for oxygen. Guide Michael Stilich

The team says goodbye to Iris Lancaster and Sandy Badillo before they head down the mountain

took him down along with two others whose health was deteriorating, cameramen Lex Fletcher and Miles Raney (who was suffering from a severe tooth infection).

Mary Ann Castimore wanted desperately to continue despite this setback. However, Nancy Knoble, who had grown close to Kearney over the course of the climb, was shaken by his dramatic turn for the worse. She told the team she felt "very compromised in [her] heart" and would honor anybody that decided to descend.

The following day, the remaining climbers packed to move higher. It was a perfect day to make the journey, and several other expeditions were moving. Suddenly, Knoble walked over to the Princeton group and told them that she was going down, that she didn't have it "left in her heart" to continue climbing.

The morning the five descended would turn out to be the last day weather conditions would allow the remaining team members to pursue the summit. The climb was over. Days later, many of the team members were still pinned at 14,000 feet by a storm.

THE BITTER AND THE SWEET

Some of the climbers found the Mount McKinley expedition hugely disappointing, and the failure to summit haunts some of them even now. Among the survivors there is a sense of a commitment unfulfilled. These strong, persevering women, who fought breast cancer with a ferocity to live life with cancer and after cancer, felt trounced by the everyday force of climate. Some have returned to summit since; many will go back.

Despite the missed summit, The Breast Cancer Fund's McKinley expedition proved tremendously successful in many ways. The Breast Cancer Fund produced a documentary of the expedition, *Climb Against the Odds*, that was shown widely around the world. ABC's *20/20* did a large segment on the trek, concluding the climb was "an incredible journey" by a group of "amazing women." Many of the survivors who retreated from the mountain in tears put a positive spin on the climb and talked about lessons learned.

Sadly, the inspirational Marcy Ely-Wilson lost her battle with cancer on March 20, 1999. Unfortunately, she was not the only team casualty. Guide Michele Potkin was killed in an avalanche while training for Emergency Mountain Rescue—doing what she did best, helping others.

The Breast Cancer Fund's team leaders continually emphasized that the fight against breast cancer was strikingly similar to mountain climbing, but the two tasks proved more similar than even they realized. The mountain does not respond to human drama and turmoil; it reflects back only the individual's ability to cope with an unmoving resistance. Fearlessness does not move the mountain; that can be accomplished only through human resilience and determination.

Left: A prayer flag ceremony at 14,200 feet before proceeding on

Bottom: Nancy Knoble gets an extra warming embrace for the inclement descent

PART *3*

MOUNT FUJI

+ **375 CLIMBERS FROM JAPAN,** INCLUDING:
Jinroh Itami, M.D.
Yumiko Obayashi

CHAPTER⁸
INTERNATIONAL INSPIRATION

+ **SUMMIT TEAM AND GUIDES**
75 CLIMBERS FROM THE U.S. (AND PHILIPPINES), INCLUDING:
Sandy Badillo
Nancy Bellen
Mary Ann Castimore
Deborah Ann Cohen
Helen Louise Ittner
Iris Lancaster
Andrea Ravinett Martin
Norma Jean McKaldin
Buhawi Meneses
Rose Meneses
Linda Rinaldi
Charley Wilson

+ **APPLIED MATERIALS SPONSOR TEAM,** INCLUDING:
Yoshitaka Fukuzawa
Luis Garcia
Diane Grunes
Hiroko Hiyama
Sam Ishii
Rika Kanda
Jerry Kilbride
Michael O'Farrell
Lynn Pearson
Amvir Sumera
Ursula Surgalski
Cathy Ann Taylor

A COMMON CAUSE

Sacred and demanding, 12,400-foot Mount Fuji became the next life-affirming challenge of The Breast Cancer Fund. Because the mountain isn't nearly as high, nor its climate as brutal, as in the previous treks, this climb was accessible to many more people. In fact, there would be four hundred climbers, all ascending Fuji for one common cause, in August 2000. The expedition, combining climbers from the United States and Asia, would effectively launch the battle against breast cancer from an international platform, as well as highlight the mounting problem of the disease in Japan.

In the last decade, incidence of the illness has increased 40 percent in Japan. Because of the recent increases among Japanese women and the stigma associated with breast cancer, doctors and relatives have not been prepared to assist women dealing with the devastating diagnosis. Patients often are neither provided with medical explanations for their symptoms nor informed of their diagnosis until after treatment has begun. According to Tokyo oncologist Jinroh Itami, a co-organizer of the Fuji climb, "Medical science avoids the cancer patient's anxiety and fear of death by hiding the diagnosis. . . . It's considered common sense in the medical field not to tell their diagnosis to patients suffering from cancer."

Itami has begun to revolutionize how cancer is viewed in Japan and how survivors there deal with the illness through his Meaningful Life Therapy. He believes that while survivors must face the dangerous reality of their illness, they must not surrender to it nor let it interfere with enjoying life. "Accept cancer and fight; accept one's limits and stretch them," he asserts. Itami had already begun organizing hikes up Fuji with some of his patients when he met Andrea Ravinett Martin.

Participants on this expedition included not only Martin, but also McKinley climbers and now Fuji guides Sandy Badillo, Mary Ann Castimore, and Iris Lancaster. Hiking alongside them would be some 70 other Americans and 325 climbers from Asia.

Opposite: Two kimono-clad women enter the Tokyo Plaza

> "In search of a cure, we leave family and friends so no one else must"
>
> NANCY BELLEN

Nancy Bellen moves at a steady pace up Mount Fuji

NANCY BELLEN

Nancy Bellen was thirty-two years old and eight weeks pregnant when she was diagnosed with breast cancer. Her doctor found a lump in her breast during a prenatal exam.

"I'm not a big believer in intuition. I didn't know if it was bad," Bellen recalls. "On the other hand, I didn't know if I would be alive in five years." She had a needle biopsy on a Friday. The next day, her doctor called her into his office. "You know it's bad when they page you on Saturday," she says.

To save her own life, Bellen would have to abort the fetus. On Sunday, she and her family and friends planted a tree in honor of her pregnancy. "On Monday I saw a surgeon, Tuesday an oncologist, Wednesday terminated the pregnancy, Thursday had a bilateral mammogram, EKG, and chest X-ray, and on Friday, I started chemo," she reports.

Then began a grueling regimen of chemotherapy and radiation. Bellen's tumor had grown significantly from the time her obstetrician found it and the time it was removed. It was feeding on the increased level of estrogen in her body from the pregnancy. Breast cancer tends to be more aggressive in younger women—a fact she was constantly reminded of during treatment.

"On no fewer than seven occasions through the course of my diagnosis and treatment, I had radiologists and techs walk into the room and upon seeing me for the first time, ask me my age, and then sort of glaze over," she says. In each instance, the next thing out of their mouth was, 'You know, it's more aggressive in younger women.' Who doesn't know it better than me?"

In response to her annoyance at the comment, Bellen says, "One of my friends suggested that I have a T-shirt made up, and while I thought it was a great idea, I was usually not wearing a shirt when this came up. So I bought a baseball cap and had it

The team at Hakone Shrine

"I grew my hair for five years, cutting it just before the climb. I carried the braided hair with me and threw it to the wind as I stood on top of the mountain."

ELISA "BAMBI" SCHWARTZ

Elaine McCarthy and others share a powerful moment closing the circle of prayer flags

embroidered with, 'Yes, I know, it's more aggressive in younger women.' I wear this cap to all my testing now. I suppose it's a talisman of sorts. Since I've had it, it hasn't come up again."

That episode is just one of several odd, annoying, bizarre, and even funny experiences Nancy Bellen has included in a collection she calls the "Lemonade Chronicles." Many of the stories deal with how she battled cancer while raising her three-year-old son, Wiley. Courage and humor were the key to her approach.

Halloween of that awful chemo year, Bellen was feeling particularly ill. But that didn't stop her from coloring an empty toilet-paper roll green, duct-taping it to her head, then spray painting the rest of her head orange and her eyes, nose, and mouth jack-o'-lantern black. "My son and I ended up having a pretty good time trick-or-treating that night," Bellen wrote in her chronicles. "He recently told me he wanted to get cancer when he grows up so that he can paint his head. I told him that I hope he never gets cancer, and he can shave his head if he really wants to. He declined."

DEBORAH ANN COHEN
Deborah Ann Cohen, marketing director for the professional services firm PricewaterhouseCoopers, based in New York, tried to spend her weekends outside, skiing, biking, hiking, or sailing. Even before her breast cancer diagnosis at age thirty-five,

Cohen put her love of the outdoors to use for charitable causes. For six years she qualified for the National Finals of the Jimmy Heuga Toyota Ski Express, a series of ski races and fund-raising efforts to further research for multiple sclerosis and the Jimmy Heuga Center, an MS rehabilitation center in Vail, Colorado.

After her diagnosis, Cohen focused on raising awareness of the issues young women with breast cancer must face. She authored a "survival guide" to early-stage breast cancer, *Just Get Me Through This! The Practical Guide to Breast Cancer* (Kensington Publishing, May 2000), and participated in The National Breast Cancer Coalitions Project LEAD (Leadership Education and Advocacy Development). She looked forward to her Mount Fuji climb as testimony to the active, fulfilling lives lived by the many women who have had to face the disease.

HELEN LOUISE ITTNER

In 1995, Helen Louise (H. L.) Ittner thought she had it made when she turned fifty-six because her mom died of breast cancer at that age. Ittner also lost her younger sister, Gretchen, to the disease. Gretchen died at forty-five, leaving two young children to be raised by their father. The disease was clearly stalking the family. But on that important birthday, Ittner breathed easier.

"I'm going to live a long time," the Moraga, California, homemaker boasted to her husband, Fred, and eighteen-year-old son, Philip, at a special birthday luncheon that year. Another time, recalling the celebration, she would quietly add a postscript: "I thought maybe I was free."

Three years later, on a Friday, Ittner was getting ready for a meeting in Carmel on preservation plans for the Hearst Castle when she felt a small, hard lump in her right breast along a rib. "Oh brother, here we go," she recalls thinking to herself. She immediately phoned her doctor and set up an appointment for Monday, then drove to the meeting.

"On the way back coming up the coast along Highway 1, it was overcast," Ittner recalls. "The ocean was rough; it was angry. That's just how I felt. I was angry. I had a feeling it might be cancer."

The news was bad: Ittner's cancer had already spread to her lymph system. She had a bilateral mastectomy with tram flap reconstruction, which involves moving a section of stomach muscle up through the body to create a breast. That was followed by months of chemotherapy and a new experimental protocol incorporating taxol, which has since become standard treatment.

Despite her family's history with breast cancer, Ittner insists she wasn't fatalistic about the disease. "My attitude was I had to break the chain," she says. "Gretchen's daughter was a teenager by then. She had lost her grandmother and mother to breast cancer. I couldn't have her feeling hopeless, believing that one day she would get cancer and die. It had to end with me. I was angry. It really ticks me off—enough to fight. Gretchen never got to see her kids grow up. She'd be so proud of them; they're great kids."

Five years after her first diagnosis, Ittner had a recurrence. She found a tiny lump the size of a "grain of sand" between the skin and the muscle, again on her right side. It was removed, and she underwent radiation.

A year later, Ittner was in the mood to "do something special for the millennium. I wanted to celebrate being sixty-five, and I wanted to honor my mother and sister. This climb said, 'Come, do me.'"

+ Norma Jean McKeldin ascends

NORMA JEAN MCKELDIN

Norma Jean McKeldin was first diagnosed with breast cancer at the age of thirty-nine, after her lover found a lump in her right breast. She was working in hospital administration for Kaiser and had a teenage boy and girl. McKeldin had a lumpectomy and radiation.

"How do you make it bearable?" she asks. "You don't. You don't. You do what you got to do. You stand right there in the moment and someone says 'you go here,' and you go there. You choose in that moment that you're going to live."

It was a tough time for McKeldin, who has always considered herself deeply religious. "I was really upset and infuriated with God," she recalls. "We weren't communicating. I felt like my protective bubble had been taken away from me. 'Course, I was fussin'. My doctor told me to get on with my life and that really pissed me off. My minister said, 'Sometimes things happen that you can't understand.' I said, 'Go on, explain it to me. I'm a bright woman. I'll understand.'"

Breast cancer has been what she calls "the pits." And even when she thought she had paid her dues, it came back into her life with a vengeance. Though McKeldin eventually got on with her life in a fashion, she says, "I stuck my head in the sand like an ostrich, hoping all this would go away."

Years later she heard about the Fuji climb. She reports, "I finally took my head out of the sand and freed up my nostrils and filled them with good clean air, and that good clean air was called doing something for someone else. I know we're all gonna die. That's part of living. But not this way. The hike was the first step toward doing something to eliminate breast cancer."

Andrea Ravinett Martin and Norma Jean McKeldin embrace after the climb

"My passion is to tranform the universe one thoughtful act at a time."

NORMA JEAN MCKELDIN

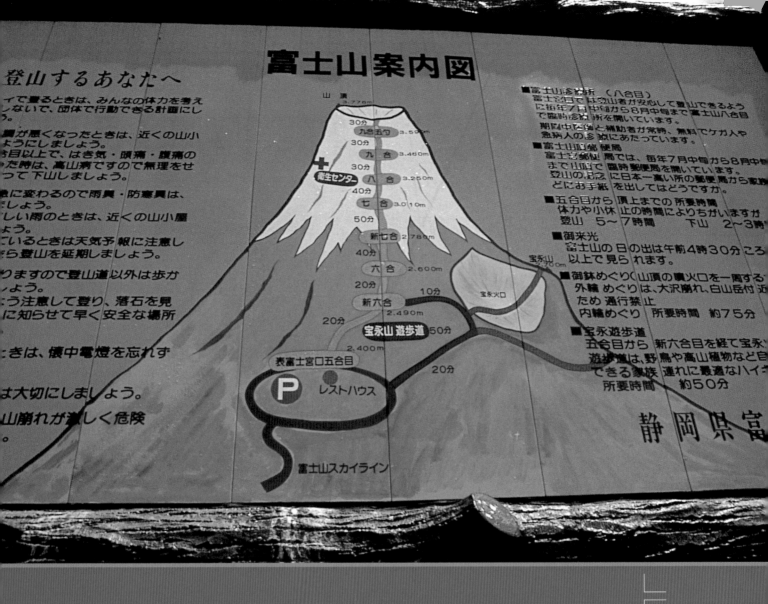

Mount Fuji route map

"Very simply put . . . I am climbing to motivate those stricken with the disease and give them hope in the knowledge that they are not alone. There are many of us fighting out here, fighting for them, fighting with them."

S. ANN DE VONA

ROSA MENESES

Rosa Meneses was born in rural Quezon City in the Philippines, the second of nine children. She joined an underground movement of student activists during ex-President Ferdinand Marcos's regime. It was during this time that she met her husband, Danny, and gave birth to the first of their five children.

Shortly after her breast cancer diagnosis in 1997, Meneses founded the Philippine Breast Cancer Network, the first organization of its kind in her country. The following year she convened the first Philippine Conference on Breast Cancer. She left her hospital bed after a stem-cell transplant to come to Mount Fuji. To Meneses, her own healing was always secondary to her efforts to prevent her three daughters and all other women from experiencing this disease.

Meneses was both a powerful inspiration for the Fuji climbers and a grim reminder that breast cancer can defeat even the strongest. A wiry woman with jet-black hair and a blinding smile, she was too devastated by the disease to even begin the hike. She battled pain in a hotel bed in Japan, while her oldest son, Buhawi, climbed in her stead. Though grieving for his mother, Buhawi, a rangy seventeen-year-old who plays bass guitar for the Filipino rock band Parokyani Edgar, drew on his own experience to console others—laughing, crying, cajoling, clowning, embracing.

+ Buhawi Meneses on arrival at Fuji

YUMIKO OBAYASHI

Following is a translated letter from Yumiko Obayashi, breast cancer survivor and Fuji climber from Okayama, Japan:

Fifteen years ago, when I was forty years old, I had a mastectomy of my right breast. At that time the shock of being diagnosed with cancer was bad, but more than that, the loss of my breast at the age of forty was so much worse. Three years after that, I had a recurrence in my right pectoral muscle and had it removed. I was quite depressed then with fear that I was going to die soon and I cried every day. About that time I learned of the Meaningful Life Therapy and learned the importance of having the spirit to fight the disease and live positively. I was able to face the cancer and began to have the will to fight the disease. I went for treatment, and at the same time I did various alternative treatments that I thought were good: brown rice diet, vegetarian diet, natural food, oriental medicine, qi gong, etc.

A joyful Linda Rinaldi during the challenging ascent

I eventually returned to ordinary life. After ten years, I experienced a recurrence. It had metastasized in a lymph node in my neck. When I look back now, I was told by my doctor that I would have a recurrence within two years, but because of the way I lived positively and with the spirit to fight the disease, the time frame lengthened to ten years. I truly feel that how one faces the disease can affect the outcome.

That recurrence did not give me much of a shock. I did not cry. I was able to face the situation calmly. I took my hospitalization as time God is giving me to rest, and actually enjoyed it. I had some side effects of chemotherapy but was able to overcome them.

This time, I am doing some alternative treatment, and am not so depressed as I was the first time. Because I have experienced breast cancer, I am able to face the fact that we all have limited time. All people die and no one can tell how much time I have. I treasure the time I have now. I do my best in what I do. At present, I am no different physically or mentally from people without breast cancer. I want to work hard and enjoy as much as I can.

LINDA RINALDI

Linda Rinaldi, a forty-six-year-old assistant attorney general from Palmyra, New Jersey, was stunned when she was diagnosed with breast cancer. "I was horrified and petrified. I had never had a close encounter with cancer. It was something I had only viewed from afar," she says.

Rinaldi's cancer had spread to her lymph nodes by the time it was diagnosed. She faced six months of chemotherapy, two months of radiation, and five years of hormone therapy. "I knew nothing about chemotherapy, except that it was something awful to go through," she says. "At that point in my life, all I knew was that cancer plus lymph nodes plus chemotherapy did not equal a long life."

Despite the sheer terror of her battle with cancer—or perhaps because of it — Rinaldi decided to make the climb up Fuji with other survivors. She explains, "I wanted to create for myself a post-cancer experience from which I could draw strength, especially during times when the fears that cancer brings begin to surface." Besides, she adds, "For reasons that escape me in the light of reality, I thought the climb up Mount Fuji was going to be relatively easy."

Rinaldi spent seven focused months training for the climb, gradually increasing time on the treadmill and on hikes with greater loads in her backpack. It wasn't easy getting to the gym at dawn before work. "Some mornings are so cold," she wrote in a journal she kept at the time. "I wonder what kind of nut I am to be going to a gym at 5:17 A.M. Several mornings I lay back down after the 4:58 alarm, but all I could think of was not summitting Mount Fuji, and knew I would never forgive myself if I didn't train the way I should have."

In another entry, Rinaldi wrote, "There are days, lately, when I just want to lay down and not get up. Today is one of those days. I would really love for someone to take care of me, instead of me always having to take care of everyone. I feel very empty." And during a particularly difficult time, she added, "Tough month—the anniversary of 'everything.' Though a bit easier than last year, when I was so off balance. This year, at least I can say/feel 'see how far I've come.' With my Fuji focus, it's definitely easier to live in 2000 and not painfully relive 1998 and 1999."

Linda Rinaldi was feeling strong by the end of her training regimen. "Less than a week to go. It's unbelievable," she wrote in her journal. "I've met my goal of 30 pounds in the backpack, and I can do 25 minutes with it on the stepper. It's amazing that the thing I despised (the stepper) when I started . . . is now almost an obsession! I have to do it! It feels great! And it makes me feel that I've come such a long way in such a short period of time."

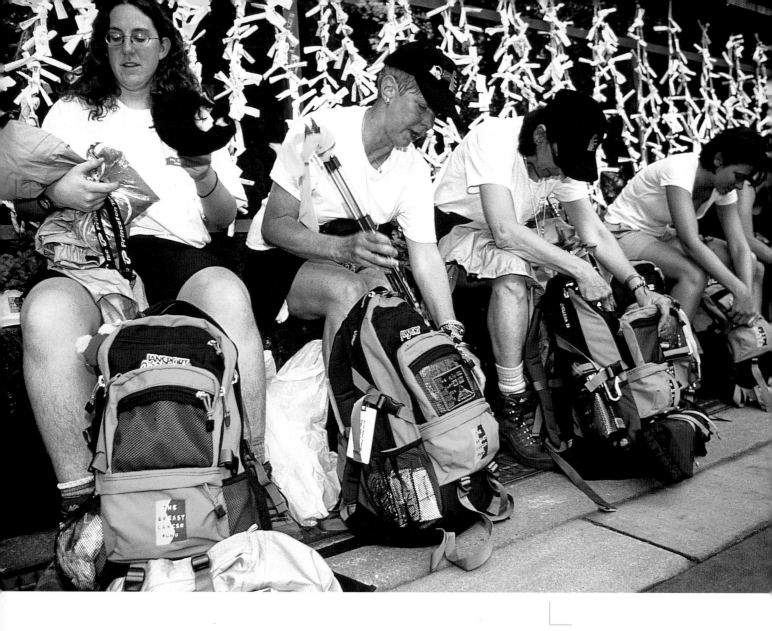

Top: The climbers' synchronized packing

Right top: Calvin, Janet, and Maclane Brady posing on sake barrels

Right bottom: Ursula Surgalski and Andrea Ravinett Martin (facing center) anticipate a great climb

CHAPTER ⁹

SERENE SISTER

FUJI-SAN

In the early 1800s, Japanese artist Hokusai produced his series of color prints known as "The 36 Views of Mount Fuji," arguably the most universally famous Japanese art. Hokusai reveals Fuji from every angle—east and west, north and south, as seen from the sea and fields of tea, from a community of timber and bamboo homes, and from the saddle of a horse. He reveals a powerful giant red Fuji, a smaller green and blue Fuji in the distance, topped with an icing of snow, and a ghostly white Fuji drifting in space. In the forefront, life goes on. Cranes preen, a woodcutter enjoys a pipe full of tobacco, and hats blow in a gust of wind.

In perhaps the most famous of the woodcuts, Great Wave Off Kanagawa, hurricane-force swells rip across Hokusai's canvas, swamping skiffs packed with terrified fishermen. Far in the distance, beyond the trough of an angry wave, stands the small snow-capped cone of Fuji—dwarfed by the violent sea yet stalwart, familiar, eternal.

At 12,400 feet, Fuji is the country's highest mountain, formed by a volcano that last erupted in 1707. It is a sacred symbol of Japan. Thousands of Japanese and tourists from other countries make the climb up Fuji annually from June to August each year, hoping to reach the top in time to watch the *goraiko*, or sunrise, which is said to resemble the halo of Buddha.

The word "fuji" likely comes from an Aimu word meaning "fire god." Priests tended a shrine at the foot of the mountain for centuries to placate the flaming deity. But as years passed, the mountain's soul morphed from male to female, and Fuji became the embodied Shinto goddess Konohana Sakuya Hime, the Goddess of Flowering Trees, for the cherry trees that blossom annually at the foot of the mountain. Each year a fire ceremony at Fuji-Yoshida in the goddess's honor marks the end of the climbing season on the mountain. The ritual marks Konohana Sakuya Hime's mythical trial by fire, when she gave birth to a son within the crater. Both mother and baby emerged unscathed.

COLOR BY NUMBERS

The biggest challenge for the Fuji climb turned out to be coordinating a mass of people from different countries up one mountain. Mount Fuji is not a technical climb, but the hike was tougher than many were expecting. Fuji's slippery silica ash covers volcanic boulders at an unforgiving altitude, presenting challenges found on few mountains of comparable size. Some climbers were turned back by altitude sickness.

Opposite: Prayer Flag Circle

To Norma Jean McKeldin, the hundreds of people snaking up Mount Fuji looked like prayer flags. The skin tones of their faces and hands were various shades of beige and brown, their jackets orange, yellow, blue, purple, and red. "Somehow the colors seemed more vibrant on that mountain," McKeldin recalls.

In the journal that she kept during her transforming climb on Mount Fuji, Deborah Ann Cohen shares her view of the expedition:

+ **5:30 A.M.** Wake-up call for everyone. On the walk down the glass-enclosed corridor of the hotel to breakfast, I think, "How nice that the waterfall in the Japanese garden sounds so lovely," only to realize it's pouring rain. Ugh.

+ **6:30 A.M.** A moment of prayer after breakfast while we hold hands and, led by our guide, recite an old Japanese saying about Fuji. The slower you go, the higher you climb. We'll all go slowly, and we'll all get there together.

+ **7 A.M.** We board the bus for a two-hour winding mountain bus ride up steep passages just like the Alps. The rain continues in buckets—no wonder it's so green around here. The mood on the bus is quiet as we all think to ourselves: Am I the only one who thinks we're crazy to do this? Couldn't we go back to that lovely hotel and soak in the hot springs?

+ **10 A.M.** Opening ceremonies. We arrive at the fifth station base area, to be greeted by the Japanese climbing team accompanying us. They welcome us with speeches, a traditional Japanese drum ceremony, and walking sticks, which we branded with Japanese markings at each station.

+ **Noon.** We're off. After a team picture, each of the six U.S. teams departs, interspersed with a Japanese team. Over 400 people in all. Not ten steps into the climb, the clouds sink below into the valley and the skies start to part. There's a streak of blue. The gods of all our cultures must have heard our prayers.

+ **Seventh Station.** Two hours of walking, lots of snacks and lots of songs later, the team is still staying together to help each other out. At one point, I take a rest stop with Charley, one of the few men climbing with us. Charley's wife, Marcy, was with the Mount McKinley group in the Climb Against the Odds expedition. Marcy passed away a few months later. But as Charley says, "She never gave up fighting, so I'm continuing the fight for her." By midafternoon I'm in pain with every step.

+ **The Eighth Station** is in sight—our home for the evening. We'll sleep here for five or six hours before rising at 3 A.M. to get to the summit by dawn.

The hike was hard, "damn hard," says H. L. Ittner. "I thought I'd never make it. My ankles, my knees, my lungs were all killing me. I'd never climbed a mountain before. Only thing I'd ever done was Mount Tam or Mount Diablo in the Bay Area. I expected some kind of hiking path. But it wasn't smooth at all."

Top: Climb Against the Odds drumming
ceremony with Taiko drummers

Left: Gail Mahoney Sherrod meets a
greeter at the airport

MT.FUJI

Top: Climbers snake along the haunch of Mount Fuji

Right top left: Mark Brady and son

Right top right: A Japanese team member (left) with Kami Lakis

Right bottom: A climber in solitude

The Applied Materials team headed by Sam Ishii

Judy Webster receives a
helping hand

A main inspiration for Ittner was a Japanese doctor, smiling broadly and squeezing an accordion while singing loudly, in heavily accented English, "She'll be comin' around the mountain when she comes." He finished all the verses, rested a moment, drew in a long breath, then began his next selection . . . "She'll be comin' around the mountain when she comes."

A group of Japanese hikers also helped by pointing out paths Ittner should take. They would hold her hiking poles while she clambered over rocks, then hand them back. "All this went on without a common word of language among us," she says. "It was all done through smiles and eye contact. I made it. I paced myself and put one foot in front of the other."

There's a saying in Japan that on Fuji the slower you go, the higher you are. If that's the case, few climbers went higher than Linda Rinaldi. Fuji was a surprisingly difficult climb for her. It was a battle that evoked the worst memories of her fight against breast cancer. Though Rinaldi began the Fuji climb with high spirits and hopes, she quickly fell far behind the pack. She pressed on, the mantra "the slower you go, the higher you get" "like a song in my head," she recalls. The second day of the climb, when Rinaldi awoke at 2:45 A.M., she recalls, "I felt as if I had been stepped on by an elephant. My whole body ached and my head was pounding. I decided not to say a word to anyone for fear that someone would tell me it was too risky for me to go on. As it was, I was slow, but I didn't want anyone to decide I was slow and sick."

Rinaldi found the final push to the summit the most difficult: "The mountain was steeper, the terrain rockier, the air thinner than it had been before. My legs felt like lead. Once the summit came into view, it appeared to be so close, but I knew it was still a couple of hours away. As I would look up to the summit from various levels below, it reminded me of chemotherapy and the overwhelmingness of it all. The mountain looked so large and the summit seemed so far away. I got to the summit just like I got to the end of treatment. I took one step at a time."

THE SPIRIT OF THE SUMMIT

+ Top: The Bunkers
Bottom: Early morning preparation

Deborah Ann Cohen continues sharing in her journal, capturing the spirit of the summit:

3 A.M. Lights on; we're up. If we want to be high enough on the mountain to see the sunrise at 5:10 A.M., we need to leave the Eighth Station by 4 A.M.

Treading step by step, breathing deeply, all I could think about was how strong I felt and how lucky I was to be alive having this experience. About 4:30, a soft pink glow reflected on the clouds below and slowly transformed the sky to dawn in the glorious sunrise.

After one more stop, at the Ninth Station, we reached the summit at about 7 A.M. to the cheers of camera crews, media, and the Japanese organizing committee members. Nearly 13,000 feet scaled in two days by over 400 people!

We assemble for team pictures and the prayer flag ceremony. We hold the flags up high and we each read aloud the names of women on the prayer flags as they flutter in the breeze—all 750 of them. People smile in happiness for their own health and cry for the losses and pain of others.

It was kindness H. L. Ittner remembers most from her climb—that, and the beauty of Fuji: "I'll never forget the thrill of looking out and seeing the clouds and having to pinch myself that I was still standing on the ground."

When Norma Jean McKeldin reached the summit, she turned to face the clouds that hover at the rim of the cone. "It was almost like you could step onto them," she says. But beyond the view were the people surrounding her and their "tremendous capacity for generosity and love and caring." All in all, she adds, "It was a great day to be alive."

Linda Rinaldi says, "Summitting Mount Fuji was one of the most difficult physical and emotional accomplishments

Prayer flags drift above clouds

"I consider my cancer a gift, a statement difficult for many
to understand. It has impacted my life, it has defined my life."
ELAINE MCCARTHY

of my life. Surviving cancer treatment and finding a way to heal was the other. There were times on Fuji when I didn't think I was going to make it. There were times when I wanted to give up. There were times when I wondered why I was putting myself through this exhausting, and painful, exercise. There were times when I wished I was doing something simple, like sitting on a beach watching the waves roll in."

Rinaldi also got by with a little help from friends and family—everyone from coworkers to her parents, who were lighting candles for her that day in church. Her life partner, James Burks, her sons Jarett and Jalen, and their dad thought of her as she climbed, carrying her to the summit.

"All of a sudden, I felt as if my feet were no longer on the ground and I was being carried up the mountain," Rinaldi recalls. "I knew I was going to make it to the summit." She broke down in tears on the summit, sobbing on Andrea Ravinett Martin's shoulder. "In a sense, I was reborn," Rinaldi believes. "For so long, I felt betrayed by my body, and then felt doubly betrayed by my psychological being in the aftermath of the chemical imbalance I suffered after treatment. But at Fuji's summit, I made peace with my body and my mind."

ONE DAY AND ONE STEP AT A TIME

When all was said and done, 69 American and 122 Asian survivors and supporters reached the summit, each with his or her own view.

Nancy Bellen had a pretty easy time hiking Fuji, but that didn't make the climb any less monumental for her. The hike and other events of The Breast Cancer Fund have had the effect of "kicking open doors" for her. She calls Andrea Ravinett Martin "the most amazing grown-up I've ever met," the first to offer her "a sure way toward healing."

Breast cancer wasn't through with Norma Jean McKeldin, though. When she returned from the Fuji hike, her mother was diagnosed with it. Two weeks later, her sister was diagnosed, then an aunt and a cousin. McKeldin does everything she can to encourage them. "I even offered to cut my hair when my sister was going through chemo," she says, adding, "I'm living proof that you can survive breast cancer. I'm a standard bearer. I'm living a productive, fulfilled life. Life is good for me. I'm committed to transforming the universe, one step at a time. I believe in the power of prayer. All those people on Fuji prayed in their way for an end to breast cancer. I believe those prayers are going to be answered in this lifetime."

Rosa Meneses died shortly after the Fuji hike, at the age of forty-eight, one day after a five-hour breast cancer telethon in the Philippines organized by the group she founded. The Philippine Breast Cancer Network issued this statement: "Rosa was out to engage the enemy and in battle, death is a common occurrence." During her forty-three months of intense struggle with an unacceptable disease, Rosa always maintained

the honor and dignity of all women living with breast cancer. Rosa lost her breast and eventually lost her life, but she never lost her fighting heart." "In all her years as a revolutionary, she faced no enemy as powerful as breast cancer," says her husband, Danny. "Rosa and I found ourselves in a war we did not choose. Only breast cancer can cause so much havoc to someone like me who lived with and loved a woman for twenty-seven years. I miss her terribly. Only my memories of her are keeping me alive."

Deborah Ann Cohen died of metastasized breast cancer July 31, 2001, almost a year to the day after completing the Fuji climb. Just months before her death, before she knew her cancer had spread, she wrote: "Even though you think you are young, invincible and immortal, you are not and nobody else is, either. Only when diagnosed with a disease like breast cancer do you learn how precious and special each day of your life truly is. I'm too busy living and have too much of it to do to worry about dying." Cohen's final thoughts on the Fuji climb from her journal:

So, in the end, have we, have I, made a difference? Only time will tell. But just like climbing mountains, one day and one step at a time, we can only hope that our efforts will inspire and educate people—one at a time—that we can work toward a day when breast cancer will be not only curable but preventable.

Joined national flags in honor of the international effort to raise breast cancer awareness

+ Left: A sacred arch off of the trail
Bottom: A shared triumph for the
Applied Materials team

SUMMIT

PART 4

THE NEXT CHALLENGE

EPILOGUE

The silhouette of a Japanese climber

"Better things for better living—through chemistry." This 1950s promise from a leading corporation launched the chemical revolution in post–World War II America. Synthetic chemicals, developed in secret as instruments of war and untested for their human health effects, transformed our lives and our environment. Pesticides wiped out countless "enemy" crops. Herbicides banished weeds from lawns and golf courses. Disinfectants and cleaners rejuvenated our households. Plastics revolutionized packaging. A better life indeed!

Now we see the peril in the promise. These chemicals are everywhere—in our shower curtains and cars, carpets and walls; in the food we eat, the water we drink, the air we breathe, the clothes we wear, the toys our children play with. And many of these chemicals are in us. For example, every child in the world over six months of age has more dioxin in his or her body than is considered "allowable" by the U.S. Environmental Protection Agency.

As of 2002, some eighty-five thousand synthetic chemicals are registered for use in the United States, and another two thousand are added each year. Unfortunately, fewer than 10 percent of these chemicals have ever been tested for their effects on human health. They have been introduced into our environment and our bodies with reckless disregard for their effects on our health and the health of the planet.

Breast cancer rates have been climbing steadily in the United States and other industrialized countries since the 1940s. More American women have died of the disease in a twenty-year span than the number of Americans killed in both World Wars, the Korean, and Vietnam wars combined. While billions of dollars have been spent in the search for a cure, breast cancer rates continue to rise.

To stem the rising tide of breast cancer, the next challenge is to uncover and eliminate its preventable causes. The Breast Cancer Fund is committed to meeting this challenge by helping shape a research agenda focused on the relationship between breast cancer and the environment and by educating the public and policymakers on the need to reduce toxic exposures.

WHAT CAUSES BREAST CANCER?

Ionizing radiation is the only proven cause of human breast cancer. Alcohol consumption is associated with an increased risk of breast cancer, as are personal characteristics such

Laurie Martin holds prayer flags
on Mount Fuji

as late first full-term pregnancy (after age 30), and later onset of menopause (>55 years). However, even when all known risk factors and characteristics including family history and genetics are added together, more than 50 percent of breast cancer cases remain unexplained.

Inherited genetic mutations have received much recent attention, but they account for only a small fraction—5 to 10 percent—of the breast cancer epidemic. Women with an inherited mutation on the BRCA1 or BRCA2 genes have a 60 to 80 percent probability of getting breast cancer in their lifetime. While families with this mutation are devastated by cancer, genetic mutation is not the only risk factor. All families share a common environment. A study in 1988 found that adopted children whose adoptive parents died of cancer had five times the chance of getting the same disease, revealing a connection to common exposures and lifestyles independent of inherited genes.

Powerful evidence indicates that some of the synthetic chemicals in use today are responsible for many of the unexplained cases of breast cancer. It is well documented that women who have prolonged exposure to estrogens are at higher risk for breast cancer, which has led many scientists to believe that chemicals that mimic the actions of estrogens may also increase the risk of breast cancer. These synthetic estrogens are found in pesticides like dieldrin and simazine, polyvinyl chloride plastics, detergents, and prescription drugs.

Other chemicals that are linked to breast cancer include the following:

+ Organic solvents, which are used in many manufacturing processes, including the manufacture of computer components.

+ By-products of internal combustion engines, petroleum refineries and other industries, and chemicals created in soot and fumes from burning diesel, fuels, or cigarettes.

+ Dioxin, which is created when plastics or other materials containing chlorine are burned, and has been classified as a known carcinogen by the U.S. Environmental Protection Agency.

+ The pesticide DDT, which is found in human body fat and breast milk. While it is banned in the United States, it is still used in Mexico and other countries that export crops to the United States.

+ PCBs, or polychlorinated biphenyls, which were used in the manufacture of electrical equipment and other industrial and consumer products until 1976, when they, too, were banned. They are still found in the body fat and breast milk of women, and, sadly, two-thirds of all the products containing PCBs that were manufactured before 1976 remain in daily use today.

+ Phthalates, or compounds used to make plastic soft and flexible, which disrupt hormonal processes, raising concern about their potential links to breast cancer.

EVIDENCE LINKING CHEMICALS AND BREAST CANCER

Powerful circumstantial evidence indicates that some of the synthetic chemicals in use today are responsible for many of the unexplained cases of breast cancer. Scientists have not yet developed an ideal method for linking chemical exposures to human breast cancer, but several types of research—laboratory, body burden measurements, and ecological studies—provide strong evidence of the connection between chemicals and breast cancer.

Because the types of evidence vary, the strength of the evidence linking chemicals and breast cancer also varies. The strongest evidence linking chemicals to the disease is based on the fact that lifetime exposure to estrogen increases the risk of breast cancer. Exposure to synthetic chemicals that mimic estrogen, including drugs like diethylstilbestrol (DES), plastic additives like bisphenol-A (BPA), polyvinyl chloride (PVC, found in many consumer products), dieldrin, some other pesticides, and dioxin may all increase breast cancer risk.

Experimental evidence links other synthetic substances to breast cancer. These substances include organic solvents (used in many manufacturing processes, including the manufacture of computer components), polycyclic aromatic hydrocarbons (PAHs, created in soot and fumes from burning diesel, and other fuels or

+ Elizabeth Shipka moves at a swift pace up Mount Fuji

Climbing creates space for quiet contemplation

"Nothing made me an expert until one day without any warning this ominous disease called breast cancer reared its ugly head and slapped me in the face."

DEBORAH ANN COHEN 1961–2001

cigarettes) and 1,3 butadiene (a by-product of internal combustion engines, petroleum refineries, and other industries).

There are also chemicals for which evidence indicates a probable but less certain link to breast cancer. These chemicals include the banned pesticide DDT (dichloro-diphenyl-trichloroethane) and its metabolite, DDE, and PCBs (polychlorinated biphenyls), previously used in the manufacture of electrical equipment and other industrial and consumer products. Although a chemical like DDT may be banned, its effects linger for years and years.

Finally, there is evidence of chemicals that affect how the body functions in ways that suggest a possible link between these substances and breast cancer. These chemicals include the insecticide heptachlor and phthalates, compounds used to make plastic soft and flexible.

WHY WE NEED DIFFERENT RESEARCH

We clearly have major gaps in our current knowledge about the links between breast cancer and the environment. Therefore, we need to focus our research efforts on areas that are most likely to provide useful information for framing public policies related to chemical exposures and our health. The types of research most likely to produce useful evidence will be those examining (1) workplace exposures, (2) household exposures, and (3) biomonitoring using breast milk as a marker to measure community health.

WHY WE NEED TO ACT NOW

While it is clear that research is needed to help us fully understand the causes of the disease, we can no longer ignore the existing research that connects various chemicals to breast cancer. We must act now based on this evidence and begin removing many of these toxic substances from our environment.

There is no shortage of advice for women about things they can do in their personal lives to possibly reduce their risk of breast cancer. Get a mammogram. Drink less alcohol. Exercise more. But with one in eight women now at risk for breast cancer, this disease is not just a personal tragedy; it is a public health crisis that demands action by all.

Existing laws that regulate the release of toxic chemicals place the burden of scientific proof on the public to conclusively demonstrate harm before regulatory action is taken. However, it may take decades after suggestive evidence is available before steps are taken to reduce or eliminate a toxic chemical, as the example of tobacco and lung cancer shows. When there is evidence of harm, uncertainty can no longer be the qualifying argument to prevent action.

The public needs policies that embrace a precautionary ethic to provide protection before exposure and potential harm occurs. Such policies should be based on a standard that acknowledges that strong evidence—not conclusive proof—is sufficient to trigger protective action. This concept, known as the "precautionary principle," was defined at a 1998 Wingspread Conference as follows: "When an activity raises threats of harm to human health or the environment, precautionary measures should be taken even if some cause and effect relationships are not fully established scientifically."

The principle is not a new concept. It is embodied in the physicians' Hippocratic Oath to "first, do no harm." It has been cited in many international agreements and protocols, beginning with the Earth Summit in Rio de Janeiro in 1992. Nor is it against progress. Rather, it is an overarching ethic to guide decision making in the face of uncertainty. It promotes a participatory, democratic process to assess and implement the safest alternatives to meet our needs. And, perhaps most important, it is an approach to public policy that unapologetically errs on the side of human health, environmental integrity, and public safety.

WHAT WE MUST DO AS A SOCIETY

Modern American life is not inevitably toxic. It is a result of choices we made long ago not to hold industry accountable for the health effects of their products prior to introducing them into commerce. To reduce the risk of breast cancer and ultimately end the epidemic, we must make fundamental and immediate changes in public policy as well as take personal action, based on the precautionary principle. We can no longer afford to wait. Below is a five-point plan that will help us accomplish this goal:

+ Phase Out Toxic Chemicals. There is ample evidence of the need to phase out unnecessary use of toxic chemicals by requiring toxic use reduction planning. Programs should be put in place to encourage, and, if necessary, require such planning by government agencies and companies doing business with government agencies. At the same time, efforts should move forward to implement the Persistent Organic Pollutants (POPS) treaty, a global treaty that targets hexachlorobenzene, endrin, mirex, toxaphene, chlordane, heptachlor, DDT, aldrin, dieldrin (PCBs), dioxins, and furans. Ratification by at least fifty countries will be required before the treaty enters into force, a process that may take three to four years (Complete information on the POPs treaty, including current sign-on status, can be found at http://irptc.unep.ch/pops/default.html. As of August 2002, the U.S. Senate has yet to vote on ratification). The United States has signed the POPS treaty and now needs to lead the way in ratifying this treaty and expanding the list of toxic chemicals to be phased out.

+ Enact Sunshine Laws and Enforce Existing Environmental Protection Laws. Federal and state governments should follow the example of Massachusetts by passing a Toxics Use Reduction Act.

Mount Fuji Project Coordinator,
Claudette Silver

Climber Sandy Badillo takes in the awe-inspiring sight of Mount Fuji

Since passing the Toxics Use Reduction Act in 1990, the amount of toxic chemicals released into the environment in Massachusetts has dropped from 20.6 million pounds to 5.5 million pounds, a decrease of 73 percent (H. Tenny and E. Harriman, A Detailed Analysis of the TURA Data by Chemical Category 1990-1997. The TUR Institute, [Lowell: University of Massachusetts, 2002], 11).

We also need to strengthen and enforce existing environmental protection laws. Existing laws such as the Clean Air Act and the Federal Insecticide, Fungicide, and Rodenticide Act must be strengthened, not weakened. Sufficient funding must be appropriated for regulatory agencies and commissions, such as the Environmental Protection Agency and the Consumer Products Safety Commission, to increase environmental surveillance and enforcement of existing regulations.

+ Practice Healthy Purchasing. Consumers, businesses, and hospitals should purchase products that are free from chemicals linked to breast cancer, such as chlorine-free paper or plastic products made without polyvinyl chloride. These subtle changes in purchasing practices will mean fewer cancer-causing chemicals in our homes, in our landfills, and in our air and water. In addition, these actions will encourage industry to provide the products that consumers want—products that are not hazardous to our health. State and federal governments should lead the way by adopting environmentally preferable purchasing practices, thereby creating an example for individuals, businesses, and hospitals to follow.

+ Offer Corporate Incentives. Companies should not only be punished for releasing cancer-causing chemicals into our environment and therefore into our bodies; they should also be rewarded for instituting new policies and processes that are healthier for our environment. Many companies are already learning that being "green" increases consumer loyalty and profitability. Offering additional incentives to corporations that encourage them to eliminate harmful chemicals in their products and processes will help them initiate new approaches.

Such incentives might include nonmonetary public awards; a labeling system to highlight companies that use pollutant-reducing technology; prioritizing green companies when awarding government contracts; investigating new tax credits for companies that reduce their use of natural resources; or providing grants to small businesses for one-time purchases of equipment or materials that would help them reduce their use of cancer-causing chemicals.

+ Conduct Community Biomonitoring Using Breast Milk as a Marker of Chemical Exposures. Chemicals from a variety of sources enter the human body and contaminate breast milk, the nourishment provided to 60 percent of newborns in the United States. The presence of more than two hundred contaminants in human breast milk provides evidence of exposure of both mother and infant to potential harm.

Breast milk—once the purest food on the planet—has become unacceptably contaminated. This argues for a comprehensive community biomonitoring program that uses breast milk as a marker of chemical exposures, establishes links to geographic areas, and initiates a plan to eliminate these contaminants. Despite the contamination of breast milk, however, scientists still consider it the best nutrition for infants because of its immunologic and neurologic benefits. How long these benefits will outweigh the risks from contamination is an open question. The answer depends on our actions.

WHAT YOU CAN DO

We ignore at our peril the evidence that chemicals are contributing to the rising incidence of breast cancer. Stemming that tide requires that we take action now based on the evidence we have now, to protect the health of people and the planet. Waiting for absolute proof only means more funerals. It is in our power to change the course we are on. Now is the time to act on the evidence.

Join The Breast Cancer Fund as we move forward to meet this next challenge. By volunteering your time, signing up for our e-alerts, reading our publications, visiting our website, or sending a donation, your support and activism can make a difference in the uphill battle to reduce cancer-causing chemicals in our bodies and our environment. Visit our website to find out how you can get involved at www.breastcancerfund.org.

BIOS

"...diagnosis is not the beginning of the end."

ROBERTA FAMA

MOUNT ACONCAGUA 1995

DR. BERNARD "BUD" ALPERT, San Francisco, California

SUPPORTER
MOUNTAIN CLIMBED + Mount Aconcagua

CLAUDIA BERRYMAN-SHAFER, Fernley, Nevada

AGE AT DIAGNOSIS + 44 years old
AGE AT CLIMB + 46 years old
MOUNTAIN CLIMBED + Mount Aconcagua

VICKI SUSAN BORIAK, Aptos, California

AGE AT DIAGNOSIS + 39 years old
AGE AT CLIMB + 41 years old
MOUNTAIN CLIMBED + Mount Aconcagua

CLAUDIA CROSETTI, Ukiah, California

AGE AT DIAGNOSIS + 38 years old
AGE AT CLIMB + 42 years old
MOUNTAIN CLIMBED + Mount Aconcagua

ELEANOR L. DAVIS, Berwyn, Pennsylvania

AGE AT DIAGNOSIS + 40 years old
AGE AT CLIMB + 56 years old
MOUNTAIN CLIMBED + Mount Aconcagua

PAUL DELOREY, President of JanSport

SUPPORTER
MOUNTAIN CLIMBED + Mount Aconcagua

RON DORN, M.D., Boise, Idaho

SUPPORTER
MOUNTAIN CLIMBED + Mount Aconcagua

PATTY DUKE, Steamboat Springs, Colorado

AGE AT DIAGNOSIS + 43 years old
AGE AT CLIMB + 44 years old
MOUNTAIN CLIMBED + Mount Aconcagua

+ End of Expedition Inspiration

LAURA EVANS, Sun Valley, Idaho (1949–2000)

AGE AT DIAGNOSIS + 40 years old
AGE AT CLIMB + 46 years old
MOUNTAIN CLIMBED + Mount Aconcagua

ROBERTA FAMA, Aptos, California

AGE AT DIAGNOSIS + 26 years old
AGE AT CLIMB + 35 years old
MOUNTAIN CLIMBED + Mount Aconcagua

SUE ANNE FOSTER, Carmichael, California

AGE AT DIAGNOSIS + 47 years old
AGE AT CLIMB + 51 years old
MOUNTAIN CLIMBED + Mount Aconcagua

ANDREA GABBARD, Oakhurst, California

SUPPORTER
MOUNTAIN CLIMBED + Mount Aconcagua

KATHLEEN GRANT, M.D., San Francisco, California

SUPPORTER
MOUNTAIN CLIMBED + Mount Aconcagua

SARA HILDEBRAND, Neenah, Wisconsin

AGE AT DIAGNOSIS + 60 years old
AGE AT CLIMB + 61 years old
MOUNTAIN CLIMBED + Mount Aconcagua

NANCY HUDSON, Ross, California

AGE AT DIAGNOSIS + 38 years old
AGE AT CLIMB + 45 years old
MOUNTAIN CLIMBED + Mount Aconcagua

NANCY JOHNSON, Ukiah, California

AGE AT DIAGNOSIS + 39 years old
AGE AT CLIMB + 44 years old
MOUNTAIN CLIMBED + Mount Aconcagua

+ Michele Potkin, Marcy Ely-Wilson, and Bethany Coates on airstrip

"I went to bed cured and woke up Stage 4."

MARY ANN CASTIMORE

NANCY KNOBLE, Tiburon, California

AGE AT DIAGNOSIS + 45 years old
AGE AT CLIMB + Mount Aconcagua: 46 years old
                Mount McKinley: 49 years old
MOUNTAINS CLIMBED + Mount Aconcagua + Mount McKinley

ANDREA RAVINETT MARTIN, Corte Madera, California

AGE AT DIAGNOSIS + 42 years old
AGE AT CLIMB + Mount Aconcagua: 48 years old
                Mount Fuji: 53 years old
MOUNTAINS CLIMBED + Mount Aconcagua + Mount Fuji

KIM O'MEARA, Cedar Rapids, Iowa

AGE AT DIAGNOSIS + 35 years old
AGE AT CLIMB + 39 years old
MOUNTAIN CLIMBED + Mount Aconcagua

ANNETTE PORTER, Surrey, United Kingdom

AGE AT DIAGNOSIS + 32 years old
AGE AT CLIMB + 35 years old
MOUNTAIN CLIMBED + Mount Aconcagua

ASHLEY SUMNER-COX, Charlottesville, Virginia

AGE AT DIAGNOSIS + 18 years old
AGE AT CLIMB + 22 years old
MOUNTAIN CLIMBED + Mount Aconcagua

SASKIA THIADENS, San Francisco, California

SUPPORTER
MOUNTAIN CLIMBED + Mount Aconcagua

MARY HELEN YEO, Cumberland Center, Maine

AGE AT DIAGNOSIS + 53 years old
AGE AT CLIMB + 59 years old
MOUNTAIN CLIMBED + Mount Aconcagua

MOUNT MCKINLEY 1998

SANDY BADILLO, El Granada, California

AGE AT DIAGNOSIS + 42 years old
AGE AT CLIMB + Mount McKinley: 52 years old
             Mount Fuji: 54 years old
MOUNTAINS CLIMBED + Mount McKinley + Mount Fuji

MARY ANN CASTIMORE, Augusta, New Jersey

AGE AT DIAGNOSIS + 32 years old
AGE AT 2ND DIAGNOSIS + 41 years old
AGE AT CLIMB + Mount McKinley: 44 years old
             Mount Fuji: 46 years old
MOUNTAINS CLIMBED + Mount McKinley + Mount Fuji

MARCY ELY-WILSON, Napa, California (1948–1999)

AGE AT DIAGNOSIS + 43 years old
AGE AT CLIMB + 50 years old
MOUNTAIN CLIMBED + Mount McKinley

IRIS LANCASTER, Cement City, Michigan

AGE AT DIAGNOSIS + 37 years old
AGE AT CLIMB + Mount McKinley: 43 years old
             Mount Fuji: 45 years old
MOUNTAINS CLIMBED + Mount McKinley + Mount Fuji

MICHELE POTKIN, Grass Valley, California (1958–2000)

SUPPORTER
MOUNTAIN CLIMBED + Mount McKinley

CATHY ANN TAYLOR, Sausalito, California

SUPPORTER
MOUNTAINS CLIMBED + Mount McKinley; Mount Fuji

THE PRINCETON TEAM WOMEN WERE NOT BREAST CANCER SURVIVORS BUT CLIMBED TO SHOW THEIR SUPPORT.

MAJKA BURNHARDT, Minneapolis, Minnesota
BETHANY COATES, New York, New York
NAOMI DARLING, Seattle, Washington
KATIE GAMBLE, Baltimore, Maryland
MARGARET (MEG) SMITH, Seattle, Washington

MOUNT FUJI 2000

JEFFREY BASS, Newbury Park, California

SUPPORTER
MOUNTAIN CLIMBED + Mount Fuji

PAULA BASS, Newbury Park, California

AGE AT DIAGNOSIS + 35 years old
AGE AT CLIMB + 39 years old
MOUNTAIN CLIMBED + Mount Fuji

NANCY BELLEN, Santa Rosa, California

AGE AT DIAGNOSIS + 32 years old
AGE AT CLIMB + 36 years old
MOUNTAIN CLIMBED + Mount Fuji

VANESSA BIKLEN, San Gregorio, California

SUPPORTER
MOUNTAIN CLIMBED + Mount Fuji

KAREN BOATRIGHT, Austin, Texas

AGE AT DIAGNOSIS + 48 years old
AGE AT CLIMB + 52 years old
MOUNTAIN CLIMBED + Mount Fuji

JANET BRADY, Truckee, California

SUPPORTER
MOUNTAIN CLIMBED + Mount Fuji

BETTY BURCH-RILEY, Alameda, California (1940–2002)

AGE AT DIAGNOSIS + 58 years old
AGE AT CLIMB + 60 years old
MOUNTAIN CLIMBED + Mount Fuji

DEBORAH ANN COHEN, Rowayton, Connecticut (1961–2001)

AGE AT DIAGNOSIS + 35 years old
AGE AT CLIMB + 38 years old
MOUNTAIN CLIMBED + Mount Fuji

DEANNA COPELAND, Grant's Pass, Oregon

AGE AT DIAGNOSIS + 45 years old
AGE AT CLIMB + 55 years old
MOUNTAIN CLIMBED + Mount Fuji

S. ANN DE VONA, New York, New York

SUPPORTER
MOUNTAIN CLIMBED + Mount Fuji

BARBARA FINLEY, Grant's Pass, Oregon

AGE AT DIAGNOSIS + 56 years old
AGE AT CLIMB + 60 years old
MOUNTAIN CLIMBED + Mount Fuji

LOIS FLETCHER, Incline Village, Nevada

AGE AT DIAGNOSIS + 65 years old
AGE AT CLIMB + 68 years old
MOUNTAIN CLIMBED + Mount Fuji

MARILYN FUNARO, Castro Valley, California

AGE AT DIAGNOSIS + 53 years old
AGE AT CLIMB + 59 years old
MOUNTAIN CLIMBED + Mount Fuji

RICHARD GELERNTER, Corte Madera, California

SUPPORTER
MOUNTAIN CLIMBED + Mount Fuji

Cathy Ann Taylor and Diane Grunes head the Applied Materials climbers

"The best stories are those about the triumph of the human spirit over adversity. These stories awaken the hero inside each of us, propel us to reach beyond self-imposed limits and inspire us to move mountians—or, climb them."

ANDREA GABBARD

+ Jerry Kilbride gives his all

Colors of our hearts interwoven
Prayer flags flying

LAURIE MARTIN

SUSAN GHERTNER, Austin, Texas

AGE AT DIAGNOSIS + 45 years old
AGE AT CLIMB + 51 years old
MOUNTAIN CLIMBED + Mount Fuji

MARY GIBSON, San Diego, California

SUPPORTER
MOUNTAIN CLIMBED + Mount Fuji

SUSAN GRAY, Walnut Creek, California

SUPPORTER
MOUNTAIN CLIMBED + Mount Fuji

DIANE GRUNES, Santa Cruz, California

SUPPORTER
MOUNTAIN CLIMBED + Mount Fuji

MARCIA HANSEN, San Diego, California

SUPPORTER
MOUNTAIN CLIMBED + Mount Fuji

HELEN LOUISE ITTNER, Moraga, California

AGE AT DIAGNOSIS + 59 years old
AGE AT CLIMB + 65 years old
MOUNTAIN CLIMBED + Mount Fuji

SUSAN KUTNER, San Jose, California

SUPPORTER
MOUNTAIN CLIMBED + Mount Fuji

KAMI LEVERING LAKIS, Palos Verdes, California

AGE AT DIAGNOSIS + 25 years old
AGE AT CLIMB + 27 years old
MOUNTAIN CLIMBED + Mount Fuji

CAROLYN LANG, River Forest, Illinois

SUPPORTER
MOUNTAIN CLIMBED + Mount Fuji

GAIL MAHONEY-SHERROD, Jackson, Michigan

SUPPORTER
MOUNTAIN CLIMBED + Mount Fuji

LAURIE MARTIN, Truckee, California

AGE AT DIAGNOSIS + 47 years old
AGE AT CLIMB + 48 years old
MOUNTAIN CLIMBED + Mount Fuji

CATHY MATSAMITSU, Mission Hills, California

AGE AT DIAGNOSIS + 32 years old
AGE AT CLIMB + 47 years old
MOUNTAIN CLIMBED + Mount Fuji

DIANE MATSUMOTO, Cement City, Michigan

SUPPORTER
MOUNTAIN CLIMBED + Mount Fuji

ELAINE MCCARTHY, San Rafael, California

AGE AT DIAGNOSIS + 33 years old
AGE AT CLIMB + 54 years old
MOUNTAIN CLIMBED + Mount Fuji

NORMA JEAN MCKELDIN, Richmond, California

AGE AT DIAGNOSIS + 39 years old
AGE AT CLIMB + 56 years old
MOUNTAIN CLIMBED + Mount Fuji

BUHAWI MENESES, Quezon City, Philippines

SUPPORTER
MOUNTAIN CLIMBED + Mount Fuji

JEANNE MILLER, San Francisco, California

AGE AT DIAGNOSIS + 36 years old
AGE AT CLIMB + 38 years old
MOUNTAIN CLIMBED + Mount Fuji

GAIL MURYAMA-VAN ANNE

SUPPORTER
MOUNTAIN CLIMBED + Mount Fuji

Climbing Mount Fuji with focus: (L–R)
Iris Lancaster, Diane Matsumoto,
Sandy Badillo, Cathy Ann Taylor, and
Mary Ann Castimore

"I climbed for myself, others, and for many prayer flags to
honor the women I have loved and women I have lost."

NANCY BELLEN

DEBRA OTO-KENT, Vacaville, California

AGE AT DIAGNOSIS + 44 years old
AGE AT CLIMB + 45 years old
MOUNTAIN CLIMBED + Mount Fuji

MARIA CECILIA PALACIOS, Buenos Aires, Argentina

AGE AT DIAGNOSIS + 46 years old
AGE AT CLIMB + 52 years old
MOUNTAIN CLIMBED + Mount Fuji

MARGIT ESSER-PORTER, Peterborough, New Hampshire

AGE AT DIAGNOSIS + 34 years old
AGE AT CLIMB + 39 years old
MOUNTAIN CLIMBED + Mount Fuji

LINDA RINALDI, Palmyra, New Jersey

AGE AT DIAGNOSIS + 44 years old
AGE AT CLIMB + 46 years old
MOUNTAIN CLIMBED + Mount Fuji

CHERYL RYAN, Crested Butte, Colorado (1961–2002)

AGE AT DIAGNOSIS + 37 years old
AGE AT CLIMB + 39 years old
MOUNTAIN CLIMBED + Mount Fuji

JILL SHEINBERG, Park City, Utah

SUPPORTER
MOUNTAIN CLIMBED + Mount Fuji

ELISA "BAMBI" SCHWARTZ, San Francisco, California

AGE AT DIAGNOSIS + 55 years old
AGE AT CLIMB + 61 years old
MOUNTAIN CLIMBED + Mount Fuji

ELIZABETH SHIPKA, Lake Oswego, Oregon

SUPPORTER
MOUNTAIN CLIMBED: Mount Fuji

WINDY CULVER SMITH, Reno, Nevada

SUPPORTER
MOUNTAIN CLIMBED: Mount Fuji

JENNIFER STURMAN, Bedford, New York

SUPPORTER
MOUNTAIN CLIMBED: Mount Fuji

JERRY STURMAN, Bedford, New York

SUPPORTER
MOUNTAIN CLIMBED: Mount Fuji

PEGGY STURMAN, Bedford, New York

SUPPORTER
MOUNTAIN CLIMBED: Mount Fuji

DANA WARING-TOMASELLI, Brighton, Massachusetts

SUPPORTER
MOUNTAIN CLIMBED: Mount Fuji

CHARLEY WILSON, Napa, California

SUPPORTER
MOUNTAIN CLIMBED: Mount Fuji

+ The victorious end

Tomorrow—Unknown
The gift of life is mine now
I embrace today
Tomorrow—Unknown
The gift of life is mine now

MARILYN FUNARO

APPLIED MATERIALS TEAM:

YOSHITAKA FUKUZAWA, Applied Materials Japan
LUIS GARCIA, AMAT Photographer
DIANE GRUNES, WomenCARE
HIROKO HIYAMA, Applied Materials Japan
VANCE HOLMES, AMAT Cinematographer
SAM ISHII, Applied Materials, Inc.
RIKA KANDA, Applied Materials Japan
JERRY KILBRIDE, Japanese Society of N. California
MICHAEL O'FARRELL, Applied Materials, Inc.
LYNN PEARSON, Applied Materials, Inc.
AMVIR SUMERA, Applied Materials, Inc.
URSULA SURGALSKI, Applied Materials Foundation
CATHY ANN TAYLOR, AMAT High Altitude Guide
JUDITH WEBSTER, Applied Materials, Inc.

PHOTOGRAPHERS:

LEX FLETCHER has two national Emmy awards for outstanding achievement in cinematography. A former river guide, he has climbed in Mexico and South America, and made an ascent of Mount McKinley in Alaska. He has filmed many award-winning documentaries in areas throughout the world, including Central and South America, the Middle East, Europe, Russia, Papua New Guinea, Cambodia, and China. Fletcher was CNN's first cameraman in the northwestern United States. He is a cancer survivor who is honored and proud to be associated with the many fun, caring, courageous, and amazing women featured in this book.

LUIS GARCIA, an accomplished press photographer for over a decade, has covered events both foreign and domestic for such organizations and publications as *American Image Press, The Hispanic Business Magazine,* and the New York Institute of Photography. He has led photography expeditions throughout China, Mongolia, Italy, and Israel, and has traveled extensively across the United States for *American Image News.*

JAMES KAY began his photography career in 1982. He photographs adventure-oriented subjects from such areas as the high peaks of the Himalayas to the lush valleys of New Zealand. His images appear regularly in a wide variety of publications including *Outdoor Photographer, National Geographic Adventure, Nikon World, Plateau Journal, Outside, Sierra,* and *Delta Sky* magazine. Kay's photographs are also used by corporate clients including Lucent Technologies, Nikon, Patagonia, Mount Fuji USA, Fidelity Investments, Motorola, Visa, Isuzu USA, Citibank, L.L. Bean, IBM, and the New Zealand Tourism Board.

ALAN KEARNEY grew up in the Northwest and began hiking, skiing, and climbing mountains at the age of seven. He began publishing photographs and writing articles about the outdoors in 1975. His work has appeared in *Climbing, Rock and Ice, Men's Health, Newsweek, Outside,* and *Patagonia.* Kearney is the author of *Mountaineering in Patagonia* and *Color Hiking Guide to Mount Rainier.* He resides in Bellingham, Washington, where he writes and photographs full time.

Additional photographs generously provided by Naomi Darling, Roberta Fama, and Tara Triefenbach.

SPONSORS

THE BREAST CANCER FUND would like to thank all of our sponsors for their generous support of the climbing expeditions, Expedition Inspiration and Climb Against the Odds.

EXPEDITION INSPIRATION, ACONCAGUA:

Adventure—16
Adventure Medical Kits
Basic Designs/Stearns
L.L. Bean
BTU Stoker, Inc.
Cascade Designs
Chaco
Champion Nutrition
Crazy Pad Covers
Duofold
DuPont Cordura
Early Winters
EFI
Eiler Communications
Elgin Syferd
GMR Marketing
JanSport
LEKI-USA
Malden Mills
Marmot Mountain, Ltd.
Mary Kay Cosmetics
MontBell America
Mountain Safety Research
Moving Comfort
Nalge Nunc International
Northwest Airlines

Ocean Designs
Outdoor Research, Inc.
Outdoor Retailers
PMI/ Petzl
Raichle Molitar USA
Salomon
Seirus
Shaklee
Smartwool
Smith Sports Optics
Sports Heat
Swiss Army Knives
Thor-Lo, Inc.
Ugg Boots
Vuarnet
Wild Country
Wrangler
YubaShoes

CLIMB AGAINST THE ODDS, MOUNT MCKINLEY:

ABC 20/20
Adventure Medical Kits
American Alpine Institute
Amgen, Inc.
Atlas Snow Shoes
Blue Water
Brita

BTU Stoker
Bucci
Cascade Design
Cellular One, Cellular World
Condé Nast Sports for Women
Dana Design
Eastern Mountain Sports
Farmers Insurance Group
Foote Cone and Belding HealthCare
Granite Gear
Health Magazine
JanSport
JR Productions
KAVU
Kodak
LEKI-USA
Lilith Fair 1998
Little Professional Bookstore
Living Fit Magazine
Lowa Boots
MAMM Magazine
McNett Outdoor
Michael Carlson Productions
MicroRents
Moon Stone
Mountain Travel Sobek
Nalge Nunc International
The North Face
Outdoor Research
Outdoor Retailer Magazine
PMI/ Petzl
People Magazine
Raichle Molitor USA
Real Sports
Sierra Design
Skywalker Sound, Lucas Digital Ltd.
Smartwool
Sports Illustrated for Women
Terramar
ThorLo
U. S. News & World Report

Volkswagen of America
W. L. Gore & Associates
Warner Bros. Records
Wild Roses
Xoom.com

CLIMB AGAINST THE ODDS, MOUNT FUJI:

Amgen, Inc.
Applied Materials
Clif Bar Inc., Luna Bar
Cloudveil
Cowgirl Enterprise
East West Travel
Eastern Mountain Sports
Elements
Farmers Insurance
Fuji Film
GORP
Jack Morton Company
Jagged Edge
JanSport
Japan Airlines
Junonia
Inoue PR Firm
Isis
LEKI-USA
Margaret O'Leary, Inc.
Marin Outdoors
Montrail
Moving Comfort
Nalge Nunc International
oncology.com
Outdoor Research, Inc.
Oxygen Media
Platypus/ Cascade Designs
Princeton Tec
Silver Creek
Smartwool
'Toray'
Wild Roses

ABOUT
THE BREAST CANCER FUND

In response to the public health crisis of breast cancer, The Breast Cancer Fund identifies—and advocates for elimination of—the environmental and other preventable causes of the disease. Founded in 1992, The Breast Cancer Fund works from the knowledge that breast cancer is not simply a personal tragedy, but a public health priority that demands action from all.

The Breast Cancer Fund tirelessly fights to challenge the myths and perceptions surrounding breast cancer while providing inspiration to the women who suffer from the disease. Through public education and public policy initiatives, major mountain climbs, and innovative "art-reach" campaigns, The Breast Cancer Fund mobilizes the public and secures the institutional changes and policy reforms necessary to eliminate the environmental links to breast cancer.

Every mountain climb we organize—from Mount Tamalpais to Mount McKinley—is dedicated to the women who find the courage to face the disease. Every publication we produce—from our quarterly newsletter to *State of the Evidence: What Is the Connection Between Chemicals and Breast Cancer?*—is committed to informing and mobilizing a public that is unrelenting in preventing the disease from striking more people. And every program we undertake—from strengthening environmental health policy to organizing International Summits on Breast Cancer and the Environment—is essential to providing the legal and research framework necessary to create meaningful change.

With this work, The Breast Cancer Fund seeks to do justice to the women whose struggle and dedication inspire our resolve. By working together, with daring, dedication, and determination, we can move mountains, one step at a time.

To get involved in The Breast Cancer Fund's efforts, visit us at www.breastcancerfund.org.

To learn more about The Breast Cancer Fund's Prayer Flag Tribute, visit www.breastcancerprayerflags.org/

THE BREAST CANCER FUND PUBLICATIONS

+ *Art.Rage.Us. Art and Writing by Women with Breast Cancer*

+ *Pathways to Prevention: Eight Practical Steps—From the Personal to the Political—Toward Reducing the Risk of Breast Cancer*

+ *State of the Evidence: What Is the Connection Between Chemicals and Breast Cancer?*

+ *Caminos Hacia La Prevención*

+ *Action Card,* a full-color tri-fold reference card that provides key facts on breast cancer, and six actions you can take in your daily life to reduce your exposure to cancer-causing chemicals and environmental hazards

+ The Breast Cancer Fund also offers a feature-length documentary of the Climb Against the Odds on Mount McKinley, *Climb Against the Odds* documentary VHS and *Climb Against the Odds* CD Sound Track

To order publications or copies of *Climb Against the Odds* VHS or CD, please contact The Breast Cancer Fund at: 1.866.760.TBCF (8223). You can also order from our Web site www.breastcancerfund.org

PHOTO CREDITS:

Naomi Darling: 101; Roberta Fama: 19, 52; Lex Fletcher: 104, 106, 107, 110, 111, 112, 114, 117, 122, 123, 124, 126, 127, 130, 138, 141, 142, 152, 154; Luis Garcia: 8, 12, 102, 108, 113, 116, 118, 121, 123, 125, 126, 129, 131, 132, 134, 136, 137, 147, 150; JR Productions: 77; James W. Kay: 14, 16, 20, 24, 25, 26, 29, 31, 35, 36, 38, 39, 41, 42, 44, 46, 48, 51, 53, 54, 56, 57, 58, 59, 145; Alan Kearney: 1, 13, 60, 62, 65, 66, 68, 69, 70, 71, 73, 74, 76, 78, 79, 80, 82, 84, 85, 86, 87, 88, 90, 91, 92, 93, 94, 96, 98, 99, 146; The Breast Cancer Fund 2000: 22, 28; Tara Trienfenbach: 72